THE PROPHETS FOR THE COMMON READER

Books by Mary Ellen Chase

A GOODLY HERITAGE

MARY PETERS

SILAS CROCKETT

DAWN IN LYONESSE

A GOODLY FELLOWSHIP

WINDSWEPT

JONATHAN FISHER: MAINE PARSON

THE BIBLE AND THE COMMON READER

THE PLUM TREE

THE WHITE GATE

LIFE AND LANGUAGE IN THE OLD TESTAMENT

THE EDGE OF DARKNESS

THE LOVELY AMBITION

THE PSALMS FOR THE COMMON READER

THE PROPHETS FOR THE COMMON READER

MARY ELLEN CHASE

THE PROPHETS FOR THE COMMON READER

W · W · NORTON & COMPANY · INC · New York

This book is dedicated
to my friend,
LAURA CABOT HODGKINSON,
because of my deep admiration for all
that she does, and is.

Acknowledgment

I want to thank Rabbi Louis Ruchames, who is Adviser to Jewish Students at Smith College and Visiting Lecturer in the Department of History, for all the help he has given me not only in the writing of this book, but in all my work in the literature of the Old Testament. His distinguished scholarship has meant a great deal to me; and his generous friendship over many years has meant even more.

M.E.C.

Contents

CONTENTS

Foreword

THIS BOOK, like its companion on the Psalms, is written, as its title states, for the common or the general reader. It is in no sense intended for the theologian or the scholar. I hope that it will not only throw some helpful light on the difficult and important subject of Hebrew prophecy, but also make more real the personalities and the powers of those great men of ancient Israel who were known as prophets.

Whether or not Hebrew prophecy marks the beginning of the spiritual history of the world, as a German scholar has said, it is surely true that Christianity as defined and described in the New Testament owes more to the teaching of the great prophets than to any other part of the Old Testament and that its followers should be far more conscious of that fact and of that debt than they have been throughout the centuries. It is also true that our civilization of today sadly needs the moral, ethical, and religious convictions cherished and uttered by those teachers and leaders of Israel nearly three thousand years ago in their own troubled times. The desire to bring home those convictions to my readers and to emphasize those ageless ideas and ideals of human thought and behaviour as they were taught by the prophets is, then, a further incentive to the writing of this book.

The Explanatory Notes which follow this Foreword will
make clear the limitations purposely imposed upon the material to be treated in these pages.

                                        Mary Ellen Chase

NORTHAMPTON, MASSACHUSETTS
   MARCH, 1963

Explanatory Notes

1. As in my book, *The Psalms for the Common Reader*, to which this one on the prophets is a companion, I have purposely avoided the use of footnotes since in my opinion they are often more confusing than helpful. I have tried to make the text itself detailed and comprehensive; and I have given in the final pages a carefully prepared list of books which deal with prophecy and the prophets, books which I myself have found valuable and interesting.

2. I have not, as I did in my book on the Psalms, included any full account of the history of Israel. I have, instead, in Chapter 2 of Part I, written a chapter called *The World of the Prophets*, in which I have tried to give the historical background necessary for an understanding of them in relation to their times. Readers who wish to do so may, of course, read the longer and far more detailed historical account in the earlier book.

3. As in my former books about the Bible, I have based this study of the prophets upon the familiar Authorized, or King James Version, since I believe that it renders more beautifully and more truly than does any other translation the various language of prophecy.

4. Readers of this book may be surprised to find presented here only six of the Hebrew prophets: Amos, Hosea, Micah, two Isaiahs, and Jeremiah. I have chosen to confine

my book to these six men, often known as the Classical Prophets, because they are acknowledged by all students and scholars of the Old Testament to be unquestionably the greatest and most valuable among the prophets, not only to ancient Israel as a people, but to the history, the thought, and the literature of the world. These six prophets were men "not of an age but for all time." Like the psalmists they burst the boundaries of their own periods and places, spoke and wrote for all thoughtful people of every century. In comparison with them their prophetic forerunners were unimportant, and their followers, particular rather than universal. It is to them, therefore, their beliefs, their teachings, their lives, their incredible courage, and their imperishable language that these pages are devoted.

5. For the selections quoted in Part IV from these six prophets I have tried to choose those passages which are at once most characteristic of the man speaking or writing and most distinguished as literature; and I have given notes and comments which, I hope, will be helpful to the reader. The selections are in no sense sufficiently complete or various to reveal the prophet fully. I can only hope that they will encourage and assist readers to continue further reading in each of the prophetic books.

6. Finally, I cannot too strongly emphasize the fact that this book is not one of exegesis. Neither my knowledge nor my inclination will allow any exhaustive textual criticism, which is, of course, available in several excellent Commentaries, such as, for example, *The Interpreter's Bible* or the admirable A. S. Peake *Commentary*, recently issued, 1962, in a single volume. I am fully aware, as I constantly stress in my pages, that it is often difficult, if not impossible, ever to be entirely sure of *all* the actual utterances of any

given prophet. Yet I am making the necessary assumption that each is responsible for the spirit and for much, if not all of the material contained in the Old Testament book accorded to him. These prophetic books are what we now have; and it is only from them as they are that we are able to gather our chief understanding of the prophets themselves and of their teachings.

PART ONE

Who Were the Prophets?

1

The Meaning and the Background of Hebrew Prophecy

BEFORE WE begin to study the Hebrew prophets as great religious leaders and teachers as well as outstanding and fascinating individuals, it will be well for us to be quite clear both as to what *prophecy* means in terms of language (that is, the meaning of the word itself) and as to the place of prophecy in the history of Israel. Our first chapter, then, in its four sections, will be devoted (1) to the definition of prophecy, (2) to certain mistaken notions which still linger about the prophets and the prophetic books, (3) to various aspects and manifestations which have marked the long history of prophecy, and (4) to the elimination of any misconceptions as to what prophecy actually meant to the great prophets themselves.

The nineteenth century German scholar, Bernhard Duhm, who saw in prophecy "the beginning of the spiritual history of the world," was doubtless looking upon it primarily in terms of time. For the greatest and the most influential of the prophets of Israel with whom this book is concerned lived and taught two and even three centuries before Plato founded his Academy in Athens and put into the words of Socrates his *Dialogues* and his *Republic;* two centuries before Buddha gave to the Eastern world his theory of contemplation; and more than a thousand years before Mohammed, the prophet of Islam, taught through the Koran his idea of Allah as the one God and his own ideas of human conduct. As to the Founder of Christianity, Jesus of Nazareth, who based so much of His teaching upon the Hebrew prophets that He has been and still is held by countless millions to be the fulfillment of their hopes, He lived five centuries after the most inspired of them all, Isaiah of Babylon, had written in sublime language words and thoughts which Jesus was constantly to echo among His disciples in Judea and Galilee.

The word for prophet in Hebrew is *nabi.* It is generally thought to be related to the far older Sumerian or Akkadian word *nabu,* which meant to *bubble,* to *boil,* or to *spring forth* and which in this ancient verb suggests the idea of speaking or of declaring fervently whatever one devoutly believes to be true. Our English word *prophet* comes to us through the Greek translation of the Hebrew Scriptures, those Scriptures which we call the Old Testament. The Greek word for prophet in English spelling is *prophetes;* and it stems from a Greek verb meaning *to speak in place of* or *in behalf of.* The Hebrew prophet was thus a spokesman; and he spoke in place of God. In other words, he spoke the words and the messages which, he entirely believed, he had received from God Himself. This meaning is well illustrated in the 4th chapter of the book of Exodus where the Lord says unto Moses: *And thou shalt speak unto Aaron thy brother and put words in his mouth; and I will teach you what ye shall do. And he shall be thy spokesman unto the people, and he shall be to thee instead of a mouth, and thou shalt be to him instead of God.*

Prophecy was, then, the Word of God, which He had delivered to His servants, the prophets, and which He commanded those servants to utter in His name. God had called them in various ways, as we shall see, for this express purpose. The people who were to hear His Word, to listen to His commands, and to understand His anger against their ways of life were the people of Israel, whom He had chosen to be a peculiar and a singular people—one who through their Covenant with Him, made through the intercession of Moses in the wilderness of Sinai, had been marked for definite moral and spiritual responsibilities toward the world in which they lived, and for a religious destiny not only in the history of that world, but of all human life wherever it was in the future to be lived. This, in brief, is the meaning of a Hebrew prophet and of Hebrew prophecy in its greatest era.

2

Since Hebrew prophecy is not an easy subject to understand in all its manifold aspects throughout the five hundred years from the Covenant at Sinai, made around 1250 B.C., to the time of the great Classical Prophets who began to speak and perhaps to write around 750 B.C., it is wise at the start to set the readers of this book straight concerning certain familiar terms and certain perhaps unfamiliar manifestations which marked the backgrounds of this prophecy.

Let us begin with some of these terms, expressions, and affirmations which, often as they are used, may well not be entirely understood.

Many, if not most readers have been long accustomed to the adjectives *major* and *minor* as descriptive of the Hebrew prophets; and they have not unnaturally assumed that these words signify the importance of one prophet as compared to another, that certain of the prophets were of *major* importance whereas others were but of *minor* significance in the history of Israel. This, we must understand at the outset, is *not* the meaning of these two words. They refer only to the length of the prophetic books and not in any sense to the importance of the several prophets whom they describe and reveal. For example, no prophet is of greater importance than was Amos. In the Hebrew Scriptures, however, compiled by editors and learned scribes from around 400 to 200 B.C., the book of Amos, simply because of its length, is numbered among the books of the Twelve Minor Prophets, as are those of Hosea and Micah, although they, too, were prophets of major importance. The far longer books of Isaiah, Jeremiah and Ezekiel are considered as major prophetic books and their authors, therefore, as major prophets, although intelligent exception can be made in the case of Ezekiel, about whom there is still much unsettled controversy, and although the two Isaiahs and Jeremiah, great as they were, hardly deserve the adjective *major* any more than do Amos, Hosea, and Micah.

Another misunderstanding is often cherished as to the so-called *writing* and *speaking* prophets. We are accustomed to say that Elijah and Elisha, who lived a century before the greatest age of Hebrew prophecy, were *speaking* prophets, as they doubtless were, but that Amos, Hosea, Micah, the two Isaiahs, and Jeremiah *wrote* their words and works. What is actually true about this assumption?

When I began some thirty years ago seriously to study the Old Testament, I read that the book of Amos was, among the many books of the Old Testament, the first consciously *written* book by an author whose actual name was known. I have since learned that the truth of this statement is more than doubtful. There is no reliable proof that Amos wrote his book or, indeed, that he could write at all. It is far more probable, according to our best Biblical authorities, that he spoke his marvellous addresses out of the fullness of his heart, that they were either handed down by oral tradition or recorded by some learned disciple of his, much later to be compiled by those scholars whose business it was to determine what was and what was not to be considered "canonical Scripture." We read that Jeremiah had a secretary named Baruch; but we do not know that the other great prophets possessed any such convenient assistants, although we do not know that they did not. There may, too, at least conceivably, have been other major prophets of Israel whose work has been lost.

Nor do we know that *all* the material in the prophetic books which we possess was actually spoken or written by our great prophets. There are, for example, in the first thirty-nine chapters of the long book of Isaiah many so-called *oracles*, which the best scholars and linguists feel sure do not belong to Isaiah's speech or to his pen, just as there are single verses and chapters, in whole or in part, in the short books of Amos, Hosea, and Micah with which those prophets very likely had nothing to do. It is well for readers to understand at the outset that even the most highly trained scholars are, and probably will always be, in doubt both as to the means of preserving the prophetic books and as to the authorship of certain portions of them. It would seem to me, however, that our far more pleasant task as readers is not to haggle over erudite questions for which we have neither time nor requisite training to solve, but rather to read those utterances of the great prophets which, thanks to the scholars, we are relatively sure they spoke or wrote and not to trouble our minds with unanswerable questions as to the material added to their books. Surely enough of each of our prophets remains to give us unqualified delight, vast admiration, and inexhaustible material for thought and for study.

Yet another idea or conception needs to be presented, even though it can hardly be summarily answered. That prophecy was an institution *unique* to ancient Israel has been, and still is, held by many scholars to be entirely true; that just as Rome produced her statesmen and Greece gave to the world her philosophers, so Israel alone gave rise to her prophets. In common with many whose knowledge is far wider than my own, I happen to be among those who believe that this statement is true: that in the greatest of her prophets, whom this book strives to honour, the ancient land of Israel gave proof to all ages of her incomparable genius. Nevertheless, it is only fair to say that certain scholars see even in these greatest of prophets a kinship with those who preceded them. These scholars acknowledge that no former prophets possessed the power of those speaking or writing in the mighty Age of Prophecy; yet they are slow to admit either that the greatest prophets were wholly *unique* in their words or in their experiences or that the institution of prophecy was distinctive and peculiar only to the land of Israel. Again, since it would be quite impossible for the common reader to enter into this tangled and obscure controversy, shall we not, then, abandon it to the scholars and begin our study of the incomparable Hebrew prophets by learning something of their predecessors and forerunners, who without doubt in certain ways contributed to their genius, but who in comparison with them were of relatively small importance both to their nation and to the civilization of the world.

3

It would be far easier to trace intelligently and helpfully the forerunners and even the followers of our great prophets if the word *prophet* were not so indiscriminately used throughout the Old Testament. We are told, it is true, in the book of I Samuel that "beforetime in Israel" a prophet was called a *seer*. Nevertheless, the word *prophet* is used again and again to characterize many different sorts of men (and women) who in their words and behaviour were far different from the mighty figures of the Classical Prophets with whom we have to do. Since this careless and perplexing use of the word is, however, unfortunately true, we shall have to deal with it as best we can in the necessary attempt to understand something about the forerunners of our great men and to learn how those great men differed from the seers, or diviners, or advisers, or "prophets" who preceded them. Nor must we ever forget in our study that far too little is actually known beyond a doubt about any of these curious and baffling persons, many of whom will seem entirely at variance with Hebrew prophecy at its best and noblest. Perhaps our task will be easier if we recognize at the start certain stages of prophecy and deal with each as intelligently as possible. Perhaps, too, it will be helpful if in our study of these stages we adopt the device of capital letters to discriminate Prophecy at its best and the great Prophets from lesser brands and from lesser men.

(1) Moses dominates the first stage and does it nobly. He is always recognized as the first and even as the greatest of the true Prophets, not because he had anything at all to do with the Age of Prophecy, but simply because he supplied the basis, the root, of all true Prophetic teaching. For it was Moses in the wilderness of Sinai, after he had known the Reality of God in the burning bush, after he had returned to his suffering kinsmen in Egypt and led them out of bondage, who gave birth to the nation of Israel. It was Moses who made known the Power and the Will of God to Israel; Moses, who revealed alike His Righteousness and His Mercy; Moses, who from the revelations given to him from Mount Sinai mediated the Covenant between God and His people, a covenant which demanded dedication and allegiance on the part of that people in return for the constant care of God.

All the great Prophets whom we are to study never ceased to realize this fact and this truth. Moses was their true forerunner and their ideal. Again and again they gave expression to that knowledge and to that faith. They understood that the most important of their teachings were not new, but that instead they had been born five hundred years before at the time of Moses, through his understanding and his genius. Their faith was, in its main aspects, the old Mosaic faith. They were but re-emphasizing it, re-defining it, deepening and enriching it, enlarging upon it, adapting it to a new age and to a people who had forgotten it or had grown indifferent to its commands. Hosea makes this knowledge clear when he says in the words of God: *I am the Lord thy*

God from the land of Egypt and thou shalt know no god but me, for there is no saviour beside me. I did know thee in the wilderness, in the land of great drought. Amos, too, knew it. In the second chapter of his terrible, yet magnificent oracles he cries, again in the words of God: *I brought you up from the land of Egypt, and led you forty years through the wilderness.* Nearly two centuries later Jeremiah knew it and based his stirring, fateful words upon it: *In the day that I brought your fathers out of the land of Egypt, I commanded them saying: Obey my voice, and I will be your God, and ye shall be my people; and walk ye in all the ways that I have commanded you that it may be well unto you.*

Moses was, then, always held to be the first of the great Prophets, his service to his people never for a moment forgotten by his worthiest of successors, his faiths and hopes their own. It was he with whom God had talked "as a man talks with his friend." Yet in the five centuries between Moses and Amos there arose lesser men known also as "prophets," although they were, with one great exception, unworthy of that term in its highest and noblest sense. Still, in the long history of Hebrew prophecy such men bore a part; and it is necessary to know of them if only to understand how different they were from those who, in the steps of Moses, were to give to Prophecy its enduring and incomparable strength.

(2) Throughout the historical books of the Old Testament, from the Pentateuch, or the "Five Books of Moses," to the books of Kings and Chronicles, we read of "prophets" and of "bands of prophets," all of whom, whether singly or in groups, claimed to be spokesmen of God, and in this very claim proved that they formed a part of the long his-

tory of Hebrew prophecy. Nor were such prophets and such bands or guilds characteristic of Israel alone. Through the discoveries of the archaeologists and of other scholars we now have learned that the phenomenon of prophecy was known in other Oriental countries, in the various civilizations of Mesopotamia and, in a less pronounced form, in Egypt. Far more involved with the early history of Israel, the Canaanites had their prophets, who were doubtless connected with their shrines and sanctuaries, their so-called "high places." The Phoenicians had theirs also. Jezebel, the wicked wife of King Ahab in the ninth century B.C., who was herself a Phoenician princess, kept at court, we are told in the book of I Kings, four hundred prophets of her god Melkart just as King Ahab supported a large number of prophets presumably dedicated to the God of Israel.

It is difficult, if not impossible to be entirely sure just what was the rôle, the status, and the work of such companies of men. They seem upon occasion to have practiced divination by the casting of lots, in which art they may well have been connected with the priests; they were given to processions, in which they played upon all manner of ancient musical instruments and by which they stirred up the common people to religious frenzy or perhaps to political or national enthusiasm. They were probably instrumental, for example, in arousing the people in the days of Saul and David against the Philistines and against incursions from desert marauders. We read that at times of great excitement they cut themselves with knives and lances. They are often called "professional," or "cultic," or "ecstatic" prophets, terms which would seem to indicate that they were trained in "prophetic schools," lived in groups or in companies, received payment for their services, and were a part of the personnel not only of Canaanite, but of Israelite shrines and temples. They seemingly possessed some sort of official religious status, if only as helpful tools to the political or to the priestly parties in power. We remember that Saul, after his anointing by Samuel, often himself known as a prophet, joined a band of them and began to speak in words supposedly inspired by God.

Among them were doubtless good and honest men who were above any sort of chicanery and fraud. Indeed, we read in the 22nd chapter of I Kings of one such Prophet named Micaiah, who stood out firmly against four hundred court prophets, clearly tools of King Ahab of Israel and King Jehoshaphat of Judah, and who said, after the four hundred had given what to him was false counsel, that he would speak only as the Lord had spoken to him, even although for his honesty he was abused by the prophets of the court. And we remember, of course, the earlier heathen diviner Balaam in the book of Numbers, who, having once seen the Lord, became a true Prophet and refused to prophesy as Balak, the king of Moab, commanded him to do, even though he forfeited Balak's "silver and gold."

These curious and obscure professional prophets surely existed in great numbers in the early days of the united kingdom of Israel as well as after its division, upon the death of Solomon around 926 B.C., into the two kingdoms of Israel and Judah. Their influence, strong in the early days of the united monarchy, seems to have deteriorated two centuries later when Israel, now disrupted into two kingdoms, north and south, quite evidently employed them more to give support and approval to the designs of corrupt or weak kings than to proclaim the true Will of God. Surely between them and the real Prophets an immeasurable gulf was fixed, as we can clearly see from the repudiation of them by the Prophets with whom we shall deal: by Amos, who scorned them with contempt, amazed and angered that the priest of Bethel should so much as *think* of him as belonging to them; by Isaiah of Jerusalem, who cried out against their false judgments; by Micah, who was disgusted over their greed for gifts and money; and by Jeremiah, whom they, with the consent of the sanctuary priests, would eagerly have put to death. And although certain scholars discern in their psychic and mystical experiences a far closer kinship with the later Prophets than many others are willing or able to believe, they seem weak and ineffectual enough when they are compared to those great men who, through their true Prophecy, left their indelible stamp upon Israel and upon the world.

(3) The Old Testament records also the presence of other prophets, who resided individually at the courts of certain kings. These men seem to have been advisers, or counsellors, or consultants to the heads of state. They apparently had little or no connection with the professional prophets, but were rather chosen because of their ability to give wise advice. Such a man at the court of King David was Nathan, who, through his famous parable given in the 12th chapter of II Samuel, rebuked the king for his monstrous sin against Uriah, the Hittite. Another was Ahijah, who warned King Jeroboam of Israel of the inevitable results of his wickedness. And a third must have been that same brave Micaiah, who dared to protest against the sycophantic behaviour of the four hundred professional prophets and received a slap in the face for his courage from one, Zedekiah, their leader.

(4) We can be grateful that the true Mosaic Prophecy

was revived around 850 B.C. in the angry figure of Elijah, who was surely a devout spokesman for the God of Israel and who forms an encouraging link between Moses and Amos, the first of the great Classical Prophets. Unlike his follower Elisha, a true Prophet also in his fight against the monstrous wrongs committed by Jezebel, though of lesser stature than his master, Elijah was a solitary man, appearing suddenly and without warning to the terror alike of King Ahab and of Obadiah, Ahab's "governor." Elisha, on the other hand, perhaps because he had at one time been the leader of a guild of professional prophets and accustomed to many companions, seems always to have been hovering about the northern kingdom and, like those guilds or bands of prophets, to be of immense appeal to the common people. Elijah bears small resemblance to a professional prophet at least in his work for God, even although he, too, may have been earlier connected with a prophetic band. His work lay in his furious strife against the prophets of the Canaanite Baals, especially against those of Jezebel's god Melkart, of great power among the Baals because of the eminence of Tyre as a city of trade and commerce. The stories of Elijah's almost horrible warfare are recorded in chapters 18 to 21 of the book of I Kings; legendary though they doubtless are, they form some brilliant and dramatic narratives by a quite unknown author. Probably these chapters are only a portion of a once far longer cycle of tales about this mighty soldier and servant of God. Yet, brief as they are, they serve to prove that the faith of Moses was still alive, if flickering, after four hundred years.

(5) The great Prophets, who arose a century after Elijah had been taken up to Heaven in his "chariot of fire" and whose age is known as the Golden Age of Prophecy, had

followers as well as forerunners. Although we shall not deal with them in this book, we should know at least of their existence in the days following the return around 536 B.C. of the Judean exiles from their fifty years of captivity in Babylon. The little we know of their work in the restored community of Jerusalem and Judea—a work largely connected with the religious and social problems of their day (and largely centered in the rebuilt Temple) rather than with the relation of man to God in his thought and in his life—is recorded in the distinctly minor books of such prophets as Haggai, Malachi, and Zechariah. Such work was relatively insignificant in the annals of Prophecy and will not concern us here.

4

It is well before concluding this attempt at defining Hebrew prophecy in its wide range of manifestations throughout the history of Israel, as given in the Old Testament, to banish certain misconceptions, too prevalent even today, concerning its meaning. What we want to know is how the great prophets themselves understood their work for God and for their country, what motives actuated them, what values they taught and cherished, what mistaken ideas they would have dismissed with scorn.

First of all, prophecy as they understood and practiced it was far removed from divination, soothsaying, clairvoyance, or necromancy of any sort. Such superstitious and materialistic action belonged either to individuals, who employed it for personal gain and notoriety, or to the professional prophets, who used its esoteric methods in questionable religious or political prognostications. Divination in various forms is commonly practiced by peoples at lower

levels of culture. It was certainly an art among many nations of the ancient world, Israel among them in the earlier
stages of her history. This we know from the Old Testament stories of such characters as Joseph, who was an interpreter of dreams; as Gideon with his dry and wet fleeces;
and as the tragic King Saul, who, although he himself had
forbidden wizardry and witchcraft in his kingdom, resorted
to necromancy in the cave of the Woman of Endor after
the Lord had "answered him not, neither by dreams, nor
by lots, nor by prophets."

Attempts such as these to fathom the future were surely
associated with earlier stages of prophecy; but they had for
the most part disappeared by the time of its classical period,
which opened about the middle of the eighth century B.C.
or around the year 750. They were certainly repudiated by
the true prophets, who scorned all willful prediction of this
nature. They were neither diviners nor were they predictors
who foretold future events after the manner of a weather
prophet or a financial forecaster. To them the future must
be determined *only* by the present; in other words, the
destiny either of an individual or of a people is, and *must*
be the necessary consequence of an existing moral and
spiritual condition. Both Amos and Isaiah of Jerusalem make
this fact abundantly clear. "*Ye have not returned unto me,*"
cries Amos, speaking in behalf of God; "*therefore thus will
I do unto thee, O Israel.*" Isaiah warns King Ahaz of Judah
that if he will not believe in God's righteous judgment and
obey His commands, then he must perforce lose his kingdom. Such prediction as this knew no chance or caprice.
It was, in fact, not so much a prediction as a *declaration* of
religious truth and necessity, a truth and necessity based
on eternal spiritual laws which could not be broken with-

out costly payment from the men or from the nations who
transgressed against them.

This mistaken idea of prediction by the prophets, of
foretelling the future, existed early in the Christian Church
and is by no means absent from it today. It is seen in the
quite erroneous notion that certain of them looked seven
centuries beyond their own time and foresaw the coming
of Jesus of Nazareth, which they foretold in those prophecies known as Messianic. To believe this is a simple distor-
tion of historical truth. The great Hebrew prophets were
without doubt precursors of Jesus, who Himself owed much
to their teachings and to their ideals and who, as we know,
deeply reverenced them as spokesmen and servants of God.
But they belonged to their own day; and their hopes for
peace and order in their own world as proclaimed by certain
of them had to do *with their world* and not with far distant
future centuries of which they, of course, knew nothing.

Another common misconception concerning prophecy
and the prophets is that the former was inseparably linked
with social betterment, with moral and ethical standards of
human life, and that the latter were little more than eager
and active social reformers. This mistaken idea arose in the
late nineteenth century when various movements to im-
prove existing social and economic conditions were rife,
especially in England and in America, and when the Biblical
scholarship of that day gave birth to the image of the *re-
forming prophet*. The prophets were, of course, concerned
deeply with the injustices of their day, with man's inhu-
manity to man. They could hardly fail to fight against such
sins since all such wrongdoing was directly opposed to the
commands of God whose spokesmen they were. Yet to see
them only, or even largely as social reformers is to obscure

their real meaning and to dim their chief and dominant concern: *the spiritual relationship of a man and of a people to God Himself.*

A final misconception of prophecy and of the prophets lies in the fallacious idea that prophecy was a form of religious mysticism and that the prophets were men given to, or endowed with, so-called mystical states and experiences, that they were, in short, solitary figures *out* of this world rather than *within* it. No idea could be farther from the truth. This is not, of course, to say that the prophets had no supernormal experiences. Like many spiritually gifted persons from St. Paul to John Bunyan they at times saw visions, dreamed dreams, or came face to face with Reality in other unusual ways. No one who has read William James's revealing and wonderful book, *The Varieties of Religious Experience*, (in which we may note, in passing, that the Hebrew prophets are cited) can doubt the many evidences which he gives in its chapters as to the truth of such revelations, such apprehensions, such sudden and intense awareness of God and of the *real meaning of human life*. William James was a pragmatist and a realist; yet he was not blind to the transforming visions of men.

The prophets likewise were pragmatists and realists who never for a moment forgot the faithless, terrifying world to which they belonged. Unlike the mystics, who have always tended to live apart from life, they lived in its very midst with their feet firmly planted on the earth and their minds intent upon the thoughts and the behaviour of the people of their day. The religious gifts which God had accorded them, their personal relationship with Him which was the one source of these gifts, were endowments to be given back to the life of their times, to the world of practical affairs, to the ordinary happenings of human experience. Their visions were revelations, indeed, but revelations to be interpreted in terms of bold and courageous action, in which they were literally *never* to be found wanting.

And finally, in this insistence on their stern and practical realism, we must always remember that, in common with other Old Testament writers, whether historians or poets, the Hebrew prophets believed only in "the threescore years and ten" allotted to men on this earth. They recognized no hope in immortality, believed in no active or intelligent life after death. Perhaps because of this stark and lonely fact their lofty and noble faith in the value of man and in his powers to make of himself and of his nation a significant part in the plan of God for all mankind assumes a more lofty and noble stature. Surely they never showed concern about the brevity and the finality of this life. Their only concern was that its years be spent in companionship with that God who had given it to men. If only this hope might be realized for Israel, the people of God, then *its* destiny was sure and certain. That destiny, the continuance of life for a specially endowed people, its deathless heritage to all humanity, rather than any future life for the individual, comprised the profound desires, even the longings of all the great prophets.

2

The World of the Great Prophets: Their Times and Places

THE LAND of Israel was already an old land when Amos, the first of our prophets, came storming into the ancient and sacred town of Bethel from Tekoa, a small Judean village or settlement in the arid hills above and around the Dead Sea. As the land of Canaan, Israel had known the wanderings of the Hebrew patriarchs, Abraham, Isaac, and Jacob, a thousand years before the days of Amos. It had known the gradual settlement and final conquest of Canaan by its own early nomadic tribes, increased by those led out of Egypt and through the wilderness of Sinai under Moses. It had been governed, or at least led by men known as *judges*, such men as Gideon, Jephthah, and Samuel, for some two hundred years until, around 1000 B.C., it had, like its neighbours, become a kingdom under three successive kings, Saul, David, and Solomon. It had defeated the

Philistines, the invaders of its Mediterranean coastal plain, and had, step by step, absorbed the Canaanites into itself as the stronger power. It had witnessed, to its pride, the growth of its small kingdom into a miniature empire under the reign of David, and, to its loss, the division of that kingdom upon the death of Solomon. When, after some two centuries of life in the northern kingdom known as Israel, and in the southern kingdom known as Judah, the Age of Prophecy began, this now two-fold land of Israel found itself facing grave dangers, perils from without and more fearful, if unrealized perils from within. It was, in fact, these dangers and these perils which called forth the prophets.

The very position of the land of Israel was a dangerous one; nor did its size minimize that danger. Its area, one hundred and fifty miles in length and some eighty miles at its widest in breadth, (an area often likened in size to our state of Vermont) was inconsequential enough. To the north was the country of Syria, whose kings were rarely averse to war or to disturbing foreign alliances. To the south lay the vast kingdom of Egypt, whose history under the Pharaohs numbered many dynasties, stretching back into time more than twenty centuries, the oldest and most stable civilization of the Near Eastern world. To the east, beyond desert regions with their marauding tribes, lay the fertile valleys of the Tigris and Euphrates rivers, hundreds of miles away, to be sure, but the scene of ancient imperialism, of wealth and of overwhelming strength, of organized armies terrifying with their chariots and cavalry, now in the middle of the eighth century under the awful power of Assyria.

Israel knew only too well that her gain in territory under David and her relative freedom from foreign warfare had been possible only because internal troubles in Egypt and weak rulers in Assyria had kept those mighty powers too concerned with their own affairs to pounce upon smaller empires and kingdoms. She knew, too, that her more immediate neighbours north and east were always ready for conflict or invasion. She knew she was what she had always been: a tiny country, now divided; a corridor between great and predatory powers; a pathway of trade always open to the caravans of menacing, greedy aliens; an inviting morsel of land easily devoured by hungry, ruthless enemies.

Yet recognition of her ultimate danger did not, unfortunately, mean realization, or the honest facing of disagreeable and threatening facts. Instead, a century and more of peace because of the weakness of Egypt and Assyria and because of highly successful local warfare waged by the northern kingdom against her nearer, less powerful neighbours, had resulted in an era of seeming prosperity for the two kingdoms of Israel. Things on the outside *looked* so flourishing that it was difficult, or at least unpleasant to discern the creeping corruption within. The old, fierce nomadic sense of freedom, independence, and responsibility, born in the deserts from which the Hebrew people originally came, had given way to a dangerous complacency. In spite of ruthless and unprincipled kings in the northern kingdom and too few rulers in the southern who remembered the Covenant with God at Sinai, in spite of the infiltration of foreigners, especially in the north, who brought their gods along with them to add to the spiritual decadence of a once dedicated people, Israel, like other civilizations before and long after her day, allowed herself to become blind to the future while she enjoyed the luxury and the ease of the present.

2

It was that spiritual decadence, that luxury and ease, which met the anxious eyes and the more anxious minds of the great prophets when they began to hurl their warnings and to utter their oracles to an indifferent and a careless people. They saw with misgiving, even with horror, that the worship of the Canaanite Baals was still operative after four centuries and more; that the Hebrews, in background a desert rather than an agricultural people, were still unable to resist the allurement of the ancient pagan fertility cults with their immoral and sensual practices. Even in shrines and temples presumably consecrated to the God of Israel, they saw meaningless sacrifices by which men sought to *appease* God rather than to *worship* Him according to the old Mosaic faith; and they saw priests dedicated not to true religion, but merely to empty rites and ceremonies.

The prophets saw, too, with anxiety and fear a new and strongly developed class system, in which the rich were becoming richer and the poor steadily poorer. They saw that the old spiritual integrity by which a man was answerable for his neighbour's welfare as well as for his own had given way to political and commercial ambitions. Corrupt rulers cultivated dangerous alliances in order to secure greater wealth and power; equally corrupt men sought profitable trade at any cost to their personal integrity. The prophets saw a longing not for righteousness or for justice, but for purely material gains which resulted in unfairness to the poor, bribery, extortion, and greed. They saw drunkenness and other forms of loose living among the rich; winter homes and summer homes luxuriously furnished; "houses of hewn stone"; "beds of ivory"; selfish and stupid

women whom Amos likened to the fat cows of the fertile
pastures of Bashan and upon whom Isaiah of Jerusalem
poured forth his disgust, irony, and scorn.

More fateful and perilous than all these wrongs, lying
behind them all as their tragic cause, the prophets saw blind-
ness and indifference, carelessness and apathy, the brazen
neglect of those vows and promises which the forefathers of
Israel had made, in her earlier days, to God. The great
prophets were not traditionalists in the conservative sense,
for they were intensely alive to the tragic situation of their
own day; yet they were always actuated by the tradition of
Israel's past, by the obligations which she had taken upon
herself through her Covenant with God as His faithful
people. It was her apostasy from that faith—a faith which
had alone assured her life *as* a people—which distressed, or
angered, or saddened them according to the character of
each.

3

Such in brief was the world of the prophets, a world
which in time was to extend from the days of Amos, Hosea,
Micah, and Isaiah of Jerusalem in the last half of the eighth
century to the fall of Jerusalem and Judea in the time of
Jeremiah, who lived and worked from around 626 B.C. to
the final conquest by Babylon in 587. To the first four men
Assyria and her terrifying armies meant certain disaster and
death; to Jeremiah, who all his life was destined to see the
southern kingdom paying uneasy tribute to Assyria and
who was finally to witness her ruin before the merciless
hosts of Babylon, Nebuchadnezzar was the conqueror. Thus
this world of the prophets encompassed more than a century
and a half, two centuries, in fact, when we extend it to

include Isaiah of Babylon, who sounded his message of hope
to the exiles there two hundred years after the coming of
Amos. From 750 B.C., then, to around 550 B.C. these men
did their utmost to make the people of Israel and Judah
realize that their safety lay only in a return to their early
Covenant with God. In terms of immediate history they
must be said to have failed; for the first four of them saw
the devastation of the northern kingdom by Assyria in 72ᵔ
B.C., and Jeremiah, who went to his death, presumably in
Egypt, upon the ruin of Jerusalem and Judea by Babylon,
knew all too well that his sufferings and his counsel had
seemingly come to nothing.

Yet in the longer annals of history they have lived and
still live as mighty men of conviction and of honour; stern
realists, yet men of vision; foretellers of doom and disaster,
yet men of hope; voices of God crying in a wilderness of
sin and bitter wrong; men of faith and courage whose words
against the indifference and the apathy of their own fearful
times echo down the centuries to condemn materialism and
neglect, of whatever age and in whatever land. They were
not confined to Samaria, or Bethel, or Moresheth, to the
narrow streets of Jerusalem, or to the rivers of Babylon.
The Books of their Sacred Law, their Torah, were later
to incorporate their ideals and their demands for men. Plato
uttered their values in a language unknown to them. Jesus
again and again read from their words and saw Himself
as their follower. The great Catholic saints throughout the
Middle Ages repeated their precepts, as did the leaders of
the Protestant Reformation. Artists have depicted them for
centuries, from Michelangelo in the sixteenth century to
Matisse in the twentieth, who placed Isaiah in his new
chapel in Provence.

In our own troubled times, when we confront dangers which they could never have imagined, their clear and bold words still sound in warning. They also were faced with alliances and leagues among the nations of their day; they were aware of the uneasy dependence of one country upon another. They, too, were beset by fear. Small as was their world in comparison with our own, they also knew the meaning of what we call "an international situation." To them the threatening cohorts of Assyria and the rise of Babylonian might were as terrifying as nuclear warfare is to us.

Their small world in its dangers and its destiny was not too unlike our great one. Yet they were consumed, as too many of us are not, by a sure and certain faith that men grow careless, neglectful, and indifferent at their own peril; that moral and spiritual laws, like the more obvious physical ones, still relentlessly operate for good or for ill; and that only doom and destruction await any land or any people who become apathetic in thought or in action toward those sure and certain values by which all men must live.

3

The Religion of the Prophets: Their Thoughts and Teachings

BEFORE BEGINNING this most important chapter of our book, it may be well for us to review briefly the main features of the preceding ones in order that we may be ready to understand as clearly as possible what thoughts lay deepest in the minds of our great prophets, what convictions and desires actuated their words and behaviour, what mental and spiritual gifts made them unique and distinctive not only among all Old Testament characters, but among men of all time. I have tried to show that, although they were not without kinship in certain formal ways with the members of earlier prophetic guilds or bands, they were immeasurably removed from such men both in their sense of true and selfless dedication to their country and in their unshakable belief that they were actually the spokesmen of God, called by Him for a definite purpose, inseparable from Him, and responsible neither to earthly rulers nor to official priests, but only to Him. A single aim and desire compelled them all: to bring home to the men and women of their age the desperate state into which that age had fallen through the sin and the indifference of its people.

Perhaps the verb *compel* describes them better than any other word could do. For they were men wholly possessed by a sense of compulsion, by a restless knowledge of being driven on and on in a labour which in itself was often neither welcome nor agreeable. They speak for God, not because they have chosen to do so by their own free will, but because they have been called, even commanded by Him to speak. Again and again they make this fact clear: Amos, who was tending his flocks and caring for his sycamore trees; Hosea, who was suffering under the burden of his own bitter tragedy; Jeremiah, who would have preferred to stay in his secluded village of Anathoth; Isaiah of Jerusalem, who was seemingly a young man of a prominent and well-to-do family and who was none too eager to give unwanted and ill-received advice to an arrogant and stupid king.

We have already learned, I hope, not to look upon these great prophets as foretellers of any future other than a future inevitably determined by a present condition; or as mere social reformers; or as visionary men, living in some remote, spiritual realms of their own. We have learned, too, that they saw themselves as responsible inheritors of a long tradition, which had been allowed to become corroded and decayed by the idolatry, avarice, and greed of men, whether of kings or of their subjects. And we have realized, finally, that they were men who saw clearly the perilous state of their world and were convinced beyond a doubt either of its inescapable and merited disaster or of its one chance for hope and redemption.

And now, having re-seen them as they were in their wider and more general aspects, let us try to understand in greater detail the convictions which they knew to be true; the faith which impelled, even dictated their words and their acts; the nature of that God whose voice they were and whose Being they recognized as the sole Reality in life. For it was this Reality which with all their power they strove to bring back to their time and place in order that the religious destiny of an especial people might be preserved for its own age and for the future.

2

The word *theology* is doubtless an inept word to use in any description of the religious faith of the great prophets. Surely it is at best an inaccurate one. For the prophets were not men who consciously formed any system of thought or of belief. Their minds, like all Hebrew minds, were not speculative so much as intuitive, not abstract so much as concrete, not given to argument or even to reflection so much as to insight. Whereas other minds like, for instance, those of the Greeks, delved into philosophy and metaphysics, were given to dialectic and to reason, compared one theory with another, the minds of the prophets leapt to knowledge, to affirmations and conclusions which to them were innate and unarguable, to truths which they believed had been revealed to them by a Source not open to question. They were not, then, theologians in the sense that they were attempting to prove the existence of God or to define His nature. To them, God was not so much the *object* of their thought as He was the *subject* of their personal, even intimate experience. Yet they held certain definite and unassailable ideas concerning Him, some of which were based on the background and tradition of Israel as a people, others of which had been born, or re-born of their own experience as His chosen servants and His spokesmen. What were these ideas?

First and foremost in the minds of all the prophets was the unshakable assurance that God was not above all else a Cosmic Force or a mere creator of the universe, although, of course, He was both, but that He was, instead, a living and a personal God, who was literally never apart from the affairs of men, who by His own choice entered constantly into fellowship *with* men. To the prophets He was alike their companion and their support. It was this sense of companionship, even of communion with Him, which made it both possible and necessary for them to set aside any natural inclinations of their own in order to labour for Him. He understood their sacrifice in His behalf, knew and was grateful for their every action for Him, had called them because He had need of them. To them all this call was at once a privilege and a responsibility. They were working not only *for* God, but *with* Him.

This conception of the overwhelming humanity of God, of His actual nearness to and care for His people, runs throughout the Old Testament and is expressed again and again by its narrators and its poets. It is, indeed, the basic conviction not only of the Old Testament but of the New, to which the Old gave being. From the very beginning of their life as a people the ancient Israelites conceived of God as a *personal being*. Almost every page of the Old Testament bears witness to this comforting, yet commanding faith. Abraham in his distant day receives the messengers of God and feeds them as one would feed any other hungry wayfarer; Jacob knows that God is with him at Bethel when he lies down to rest; Deborah knows that God is coming from Sinai to aid her and Barak in their stand against the Canaanites; Job, although he cannot understand the mysterious ways of God, is so conscious that He is with men that he dares to argue with Him, even to upbraid Him, as is Abraham conscious of the same truth when he pleads with God to spare a city, even though it has only ten righteous men within it. To upbraid God, to argue and plead with Him, means to them both their close fellowship with Him. Moses talks with God. So does Elijah, four hundred years after Moses, and he, too, in the shadow of Mount Sinai. The psalmists know that He is the strength of their hearts and their portion forever.

This idea of active participation in the daily affairs of men, this common life shared by God and His people, is emphasized by all the prophets, who in their concrete, personal metaphors see Him always as inseparable from the homely actions and happenings of daily life. To Hosea, He takes a child by the arms so that he may learn to walk; to Amos, He is a farmer, pressing down sheaves in a cart or sifting the grains of corn in a sieve, or He is a builder dropping a plumb-line to measure His work; to Jeremiah, He writes His words in the hearts of men as a scribe writes words upon a scroll; to Isaiah of Jerusalem, God sees His people as the familiar ox and the ass, who are dependent upon their owners for their care just as God's people are dependent upon Him; to both Isaiah and Jeremiah, He is a fuller washing away common dirt with soap; to Isaiah of Babylon, He takes upon Himself the homely figure of the water-seller, calling his wares in the town market-place. Perhaps, indeed, the prophets are even more concrete and direct in this expression of participation and companionship than are any other writers of the Old Testament; for they affirm that God is again calling His people into this neglected relationship of intimacy so that that people may once more be restored to its place in the family of God.

This family relationship is made both close and clear by the figure of the *redeemer*, which the earlier prophets, Hosea, Micah, and Isaiah of Jerusalem, use and which, with its accompanying imagery and symbolism, becomes perhaps the most important theme in the prophetic poetry of Isaiah of Babylon. In ancient Israel a redeemer was the nearest kinsman, who assured the wholeness and the continuance of his family by the redemption of that which had once belonged to it, whether a slave, a relative, or a piece of property. Thus, in the story of Ruth, Boaz is the redeemer, who buys Naomi's land and that of Ruth in order to keep intact the family inheritance. No word applied to God could better suggest the family relationship which was so deeply revered in Israel and of which all the prophets were so constantly aware.

If God, then, is to the prophets a husband and a father, and if, through her sinful forgetfulness, Israel has become a faithless wife and an erring daughter, God naturally possesses those attributes which men on earth possess in their own family relationships. Human emotions are, therefore, neither unfamiliar nor unfelt by Him. He can be indignant and angry as well as forbearing and compassionate, impatient and patient, sorrowful and glad, displeased and approving. He knows and is moved by all the rightful and natural emotions by which men are moved.

For the Hebrew prophets, then, knowledge of God was

no matter of detached, intellectual understanding, but rather one of personal, revealing relationship. They were convinced that because of this knowledge of Him they stood in His intimate counsel; could understand His demands, His disappointments, His anger; could work *with* Him in His hopes and desires for men. And from this knowledge and this conviction arose inevitably the second of their ideas and conceptions: the faith that God, who is Himself Righteousness and Justice, demands of men the best of which they are capable—in other words, moral righteousness in their daily lives, in their dealings one with another.

This moral righteousness had been forgotten by Israel, had given place alike to idolatry in worship and to selfishness and injustice in human affairs. To the prophets this backsliding was religious apostasy because it both disrupted the life of God's people and denied His rule as the God of Righteousness. Nor was this righteousness to them any abstract quality of God. Instead, like His humanity, it was, and must be, concretely and directly operative in the daily decisions of men.

They were often violent in their words because they saw honesty and justice forgotten and violated by a people whose forefathers had made a solemn Covenant with God—a covenant which by their own free will had bound and pledged them to acts of mercy and compassion, to moral uprightness in life. Nor was righteousness in the minds of the prophets only an obligation imposed by God upon a people as a religious duty. It was, quite simply, religion itself, the sole way by which a man might know and serve God, might enter into fellowship with Him, might become His friend and His companion, a member of His family. Micah, or perhaps a disciple of his, makes this fact abundantly clear when he gives his definition of this religion: *And what doth the Lord require of thee, but to do justly, and to love mercy, and to walk humbly with thy God?*

These ideas of the prophets, that God is a *personal* God, an active and eager participant in all the affairs of men, and that He not only demands righteousness in human life, but is Himself that Righteousness, were, of course, in no sense new ideas. They had been explicit and intrinsic in the long life of Israel as a people. Yet they had never since the days of Moses been declared as the prophets declared them. In the teachings, the inspired utterances of these men, they were re-born to such an extent that they became new and vibrant, much as some long-forgotten, long-hidden object or thought suddenly becomes new upon discovery, its meaning once more real, its value multiplied a thousandfold.

3

Among the ideas inherited by the prophets from the background and the long tradition of Israel was the idea of God as the God of history. This idea, next in importance to those of His *personal* relationship with men and of that *righteousness* which He Himself not only possesses, but *is*, lies behind and within all prophetic teaching, just as it forms the basis of all Old Testament faith. We must, indeed, remember always that to the devout Hebrew mind history was inseparable from religion. There was no history of Israel without religion; there could be, for Israel, no religion apart from history. The two were one, an entity, indivisible. The active manifestation of the presence of God through historical events is not only at the root of the religion of ancient Israel; there is no religion without it.

This wholly religious understanding and interpretation

of history was unique and peculiar to the people of Israel. Nothing like it was known to other ancient religions, which were based not upon history, but rather upon the physical processes of Nature, upon the ideas of fertility, growth, and harvest, the death of the earth at the close of the year and its resurrection in the spring, the recurrent cycle of the seasons. These statements do not mean that upon occasion the gods of other nations might not be accredited with power over events—for example, with the winning of victory for their people. We know, to cite two illustrations, that Chemosh, the god of Moab, is thanked for restoring his land after its conquest by Israel, and that Marduk, the god of the Babylonians, is characterized as the friend of Cyrus, whom he has called to conquer Babylon. Yet these are but isolated incidents and do not in any way resemble the *complete* view of history which was unique to Israel.

The Old Testament is marked throughout by the historical quality both of its thought and of its material. It is built around the history, the course of events, in the life of a people; and we can never understand it unless, and until we recognize this fact. The prophets, like other Old Testament writers, believed and taught that God had revealed Himself to Israel by the events of her history, events designed and carried out by Him; and they are always seeking for ways and means to bring this belief back to a people who had either forgotten it or were grossly misinterpreting it. Amos and Hosea are horrified when they see on every side the idolatrous practices of the northern kingdom, because they discern in such practices the knowledge that Israel has either forgotten her historical inheritance or that she is falsely assuming that God must favour her in the present as He has done in the past, however much she has turned away from that past. Amos cries out that the *Day of the Lord*, which Israel is blindly expecting to add to her political and economic prosperity, can be but a day of judgment and of punishment, a Day of Doom. Hosea, more than any other of the prophets, is revolted by the practice of Canaanitish rites which he sees on every side, because to him such idolatry is proof that Israel has forsaken the old knowledge and revelation given her by God in her desert wanderings after her freedom from Egyptian bondage.

This unique conception of history and religion we may define as a *linear* conception to distinguish it from the *cyclic* conceptions of other ancient peoples. Had the prophets made an image of it, pictured it in any concrete, visual sense, such an image might well have been a long, straight horizontal line. Even such a simple image, however, would have been impossible to construct and even more impossible to conceive since it began at the beginning of time and stretched onward toward an unknown and illimitable future when God's purposes for His own people and for all the peoples of the world should at last be fulfilled. Such an imaginary line can best be defined, perhaps, in the beautiful and mysterious words of Psalm 90, as leading "from everlasting to everlasting."

To Israel and to her great prophets this long line of history (after God's creation of the world and after numberless other events lost in the abysses of time) had become marked, or punctuated, by certain happenings known to them as the Acts of God toward His chosen people, a people whom He had chosen in order that they might make known His Will for all mankind. It was God, who had sent Abraham out of Ur of the Chaldees into the land of Canaan; God, who had led the descendants of the patriarchs into the

land of Egypt for grass and for water in a time of famine;
God, who had delivered them by the hand of Moses out
of oppression under the Pharaoh; and God, who had cared
for them in the wilderness before they had entered their
Promised Land, given them by Him. It was God, who had
sworn not only to reward them according to their righteous
acts and their continued faith in Him, but to punish them
for their sins against Him and against their fellowmen,
even against the stranger within their gates.

God was, then, to the prophets, as He had been for five
long centuries in the minds of their countrymen, the God of
history, of human events and of human experience. From
the remotest beginnings of that history to its unforeseen
end in some far distant future, He *has been, is*, and *will be*
in supreme control. This conviction was surely fundamental
to their faith; and yet, as with all their convictions and
teachings, they threw over it a new light, an illumination
which sharpened its outlines and revealed its deepest mean-
ings, brought out its darkness and its shadows.

From Amos to Jeremiah, although all recognize the stu-
pendous work of God for the sake of Israel in the past, it is
her problematical present with which they are most deeply
concerned. Inheritors of a tradition they surely are; but yet
they are also stern and uncompromising revealers of a destiny. Their very faith in the closeness of God to His people,
in His demands upon them *as* His people, makes it impossible for them to rely upon the sure and certain continuance
of His favour. To them the present condition of Israel,
because of her idolatry, her complacency and prosperity,
her sins against herself, her countrymen, and her God, is
in peril from His righteous judgment. They know that
through history God is one day to establish His sovereignty;

therefore, they understand that nothing which has to do with the moral and spiritual value of men can be of indifference to Him. Instead, every action must weigh for good or for ill, supply its link in the great chain of history, work either for or against the people of Israel. There can be no clinging to a precedent once bestowed, no reliance upon God's favour in the past, unless righteousness and justice ensure that favour for the future.

This understanding of the prophets—that God, eternally just, can punish as well as reward and that upon the moral decisions of men their fate inevitably depends—resulted in the strength and power with which all of them demand a decision for right or for wrong. Such power is shown in the threats which Amos hurls against the priest Amaziah of Bethel and against King Jeroboam and his sinful kingdom, which Isaiah of Jerusalem, in his turn, hurls against King Ahaz of Judah, and which Jeremiah, more than a century later, cries out against the wickedness and the weakness of King Jehoiakim and King Zedekiah. History, they all know, is determined for good or for ill only by means of the relationship between a people and its God.

4

If the best scholars are right—and who would want to doubt them?—in claiming that Amos himself is not the author of the lovely verse in his 5th chapter, a verse in which the writer urges the careless people of the northern kingdom to "seek him that maketh the seven stars and Orion," he most surely had ample occasion in his life to look upon the Pleiades and the Mighty Hunter in his familiar desert skies. He had constant occasion, too, to think upon that God who had formed his mountains and hills and made "the darkness of the early morning." Hosea, like Amos, was a man of the country and also uses country images: the dew upon the grass, the clouds, the lilies of the fields, the olive trees, the scent of the cedars. Isaiah of Jerusalem, always a man of the city, is keenly aware also of the vineyards, the gardens about Jerusalem, the oak trees; and Jeremiah never forgets the birds, the partridge, the stork, the crane, and the swallow. All of them leave to Isaiah of Babylon the fuller description of God's creation; and yet all clearly discern and reverence Him as the Maker of the Universe, although the full and explicit story of that creation as given in the first chapter of Genesis was written long after their day. The things which they saw about them were in themselves responsible for their obvious sensitiveness to the manifold works of God in nature.

Always to the prophets, as we have seen, the chief attributes of God are His personal concern for men and His righteousness; and in this emphasis, renewed, even re-made by their genius, they are not removed from Old Testament thought in general. Even after the story of God's creation of the world took definite literary form in the first chapter of Genesis, it always held a relatively secondary place in the thought and the teaching of Israel. It was an idea, not in any sense unique to Israel as was the idea of God as the God of history. Instead, it was common to other ancient peoples, who were accustomed to ascribe to their gods the miracles of light and darkness, land and sea, moon and stars. Devout Hebrews from their earliest narrators to their latest poets never believed in God merely *because they saw the wonders of His creation*. Rather, they accepted and gratefully acknowledged these wonders *because they believed in Him*. To them all, as surely to the prophets also, God had made the world, not primarily for itself and its wonders, but for the sake of man, as the place where man could fulfill God's purposes for all men, as the setting for the drama of human life.

It would, then, be a mistake to look upon the creation of the universe, at least in the details so familiar to us from the Genesis story, as any inherited idea of the prophets, for in their day it was *not* an inherited idea, one long stressed in tradition as was the idea of God's work in history. And yet, it seems to me, it would be equally a mistake to fail to realize the extreme sensitiveness which they possessed (and which they constantly illustrate in imagery and symbol) toward the works of God in His world, works toward which they are never careless, indifferent, or unobservant as we shall see when we study them more carefully, both as individuals and as literary artists.

5

And now to conclude our study of the teachings and the convictions of the great prophets, we must become aware of certain other ideas—ideas which are perhaps not so basic to prophetic teaching as those already given, but which are, nevertheless, necessary for any clear understanding of the prophets themselves as moral and spiritual leaders. Shall we, then, consider three of these further ideas? Two of them are concrete and direct. The third is less easy to define; and yet to the individual it is of the utmost importance since it not only lies at the very heart of Hebrew prophecy, but also concerns every man in his thoughts and his values.

To consider the first of these further and final ideas: What did the prophets think and teach about *sin?* How did they define it?

Sin, of course, must in general be defined according to the nature of the god whom one sins against. This statement may at first sound difficult; but its meaning is very easy to grasp. To illustrate: If the god whom one worships demands, because of his nature and character, ritual and ceremonial, then one sins in withholding these from him. If he demands material sacrifices, from fields or from flocks, then such sacrifices must be given him. If he demands observances of certain days, or of certain fasts or feasts, sacred to him, then the failure to observe such days constitutes a sin against him.

This teaching is always implicit and often explicit in all prophetic teaching. To the great prophets of Israel, as we have seen, God demands none of these things. Instead, He demands righteousness of life; therefore, to them any form of cruelty, injustice, or even callousness toward one's fellowman is sin, a religious offence, an act of *rebellion* against both the commands and the nature of God.

In the thought of the prophets sin should never be defined merely as a wrong act, or even as the sum of many wrong acts. These acts were plentiful enough in the life of Israel which they saw about them: avarice, treachery, gross materialism, sensuality, cruelty, injustice, idolatry. Yet these were the inevitable *results* and *consequences* of sin. Sin itself to them is a state of the human mind, a state of mind which no longer recognizes God—a condition of estrangement from Him or of rebellion against Him.

Perhaps sin with all its inescapable wrongs can best be defined in its prophetic sense as this rebellion. Isaiah of Jerusalem uses the word to excellent effect when he cries in the words of God: *I have nourished and brought up children, and they have rebelled against me.* And Hosea makes use of the same word to describe the desolation which must come to Samaria because *she hath rebelled against her God*.

To Jeremiah sin has the connotation not only of *rebellion*, although he, too, uses the word, but of *forsaking*. He who was perhaps the most sensitive of all the prophets, who was himself forsaken, who suffered most acutely because in his own devotion to God he could never comprehend the indifference of men, interprets sin as the willful turning away from God, forsaking Him as one cruelly forsakes a member of one's family, or a true friend, or as one carelessly surrenders an old and cherished ideal or principle.

All the prophets exhaust the resources of their language in their fervent attempts to bring home to Israel the meaning of her *rebellion* against God, her *forsaking* of Him. Metaphors and images are constantly on their lips, familiar, homely images which seemingly should lie deep in the comprehension of their listeners because they are gathered from familiar, homely experience. To Isaiah of Jerusalem, in the language of the physician, Israel is like a person sick from wounds and bruises, or, in the language of the gardener, she is like a deserted cottage over-run by gourds; to Amos, in the language of the countryman, she is like a man fleeing in terror from a lion only to meet a bear or a deadly serpent; to Jeremiah, in the language of the shepherd, she is like a sheep that is lost; to Hosea, in the language of a father, she is again and again like an erring and disobedient child or like a wayward son who has broken his father's heart. By such vivid analogies as these they strive to make real the rebellion of Israel.

Isaiah of Jerusalem, alone among the prophets of his time (by which prophets we mean Amos, Hosea, and Micah) stresses yet another idea and conception of God: His holiness and His terrible majesty. To this Isaiah He is repeatedly the *Holy One of Israel,* the King of kings, the Lord of hosts; and he constantly makes use of these exalted terms to describe the nature of God. This conception of God which seems to emphasize His *remoteness* from man, His *might,* His *awfulness,* His *unfathomable mystery,* may well be thought of as paradoxical, almost contradictory, when placed side by side with His personal concern for men, His closeness, even His intimacy. Yet although this holiness, this mystery, is not stressed by the contemporaries of Isaiah of Jerusalem, it finds expression in several of the psalms; it is the subject of many of the poems of Isaiah of Babylon, who, as we shall see, repeats the very epithets used by the earlier Isaiah; Job is overwhelmed by it in the book called by his name; and some of the most beautiful portions of the book of Proverbs, portions which describe the nature of Wisdom, surely emphasize it.

All these writings are later in time than are the utterances of the prophets; and yet long before the days of Isaiah of Jerusalem this two-fold nature of God, His closeness and His remoteness, His intimacy and His mystery, had surely been recognized in Old Testament tradition and story. Nor could it have seemed contradictory or paradoxical to those Old Testament characters who quite obviously understood their God as possessing both qualities. Else how could Moses talk with God as with a friend and at the same time discern His awful majesty at Mount Sinai, see His holiness in the burning bush and yet listen to His words as to the words of a companion? How could Abraham recognize with awe God's terrible command to him to sacrifice his only son Isaac, and yet upon another occasion feel fa-

miliar enough with Him to argue and to plead with Him?
How could Jacob describe Bethel in the darkness of the
night as *dreadful* because of the presence of the Lord, and
yet, when he wrestled with the angel of God, refuse to let
that angel go from him without a blessing? How could
Elijah know that God was speaking to him in "a still, small
voice" rather than in the wind, the earthquake, and the fire
through which he was expecting Him to speak, in a place
long recognized as a holy place?

So Isaiah of Jerusalem was in no sense alone in his dis-
cernment of the holiness, the awful majesty of God. It had
been felt long before his day by the Old Testament patriarchs and by former, earlier prophets. Nor is Isaiah himself overwhelmed by God's holiness in itself when in his
Temple vision he sees "the Lord, high and lifted up." Instead, his almost instant reaction is a sense of his own unworthiness as a man and of the sinfulness of the people
among whom he dwells. How is it, he wonders, that he, "a
man of unclean lips," can have been granted a vision of the
Most High? In other words, he transforms the *holiness of*
God into a more exalted *righteousness*. This is what he
means when he says later in his book: *God that is holy*
shall be sanctified in righteousness.

This seeming paradox, then, of the nature of God is not
really a paradox in the Old Testament mind. God is perfect; man is imperfect; God is spirit; man is bound to earth.
Yet of God's goodness and mercy, themselves attributes of
His holiness, He is a friend to man, yearns over him, awaits
his perfection as man. *As for God, his way is perfect*, writes
the psalmist; yet, *he is a buckler to all those who trust in*
him.

To Isaiah of Jerusalem, the one among the prophets who

is most keenly aware of the holiness of God, this very holiness makes man more aware of his own unworthiness, fills him with a sense of the necessity for worship, and yet fires him with an eagerness to fulfill God's commands. It exalts God, to be sure, and yet it brings Him into closer communion with His servants. His holiness is to be reverenced, even feared *as* holiness; nevertheless, it must forever be allied with human endeavour and with human responsibility. It can never be seen apart from that responsibility, as this Isaiah understood even in the midst of his awe and wonder.

The culminating idea of the great prophets, and the most profound legacy of that prophecy to men of every age, is their conception of a man's religion as related to his life, their conviction that no truly rich and complete life *can* be experienced apart from religion, away from God. This was not a new idea. It had existed since the days of Moses and the Covenant in the wilderness, perhaps even centuries before, if we can trust persistent tradition. But in the world of the prophets, a world disrupted by economic, social, and political conflict, by idolatry, dangerous prosperity, and sordid materialism, it had become tarnished and languid; its vitality had been lost, its meaning dimmed. The prophets gave it new reality, insisted upon its necessity, gave, or strove to give it a new sense of unity; that is, of wholeness, of completeness. Religion to them was not only the very core of their own existence; it must be, they understood, the only true life of men. *It was this persistent, active inculcation of a spiritual meaning into every aspect, however small, of human life which underlay all their teachings.*

To them, literally nothing in man's experience can be seen clearly, apart from God. All thoughts must be related to Him; all decisions must be made in the light of His desires and commands; even the smallest of acts must be performed according to those spiritual values which He has decreed for men. Such thoughts, decisions, and behaviour cannot, of course, be separated from life in human society. It, too, must be shaped and ordered by them.

And yet, to the prophets, religion is, first of all, like sin, a *state of mind,* never passive, but always active, the dedication of the spirit and the soul of man only to the highest and noblest thoughts, perceptions, and desires. Just as God is to be feared and worshipped, not because of what He can *do* for man, but for what He *is,* so to the prophets a man's life on this earth must be seen for what it is: a brief span of years to be lived either *without* the constant awareness of the presence of God or *with* that transforming, transcending awareness. Amos brings this conviction from the austerity of the desert; Hosea, from his own sorrow; Micah, from the sufferings of his fellow countrymen; Isaiah of Jerusalem, from his vision in the Temple; Jeremiah, from his bitter loneliness; Isaiah of Babylon, from his new hope.

Like one of our modern philosophers all the prophets might have said and, indeed, did say, each in his own words: *The task of man is to become what he already is.* They knew and unceasingly taught that man is the child and the servant of God, and that in every aspect of his life he can be directed and defended only by his sense of that Reality, consumed only by that Knowledge, sustained only by that indispensable Vision.

6

And finally, in any study of the Hebrew prophets we must never forget that they were men of their own time, made by its urgencies, intent upon its needs. They spoke to their own disturbed age; and we must never completely isolate them from that age or think that they, being human, were incapable of errors or of mistakes. They live today because their faith and their teachings, even although these arose from special conditions, had to do with eternal truths.

Out of their immediate situations, their particular problems, they forged universal and permanent Realities. Like other great thinkers and writers throughout the ages, from Homer, Plato, and Virgil to Dante, Shakespeare, and Milton, they became detached from their own times to become the permanent heritage of mankind, simply because of the universal nature of their thought, the eternal value of their words.

If we seek for a phrase which describes them all, for words which define the spiritual pattern of their prophecy, perhaps we cannot do better than to say that *their dynamic and lasting power lay in their new understanding and revelation of the Truth and the Reality of God.*

PART TWO

The Prophets as Men

BEFORE THE readers of this book begin to see our six prophets as individuals, each influenced, even to a large extent *made* by the circumstances peculiar to his own background and by traits characteristic only of him, I should like to make clear the methods and the aims which must govern these portraits. Scholars, of course, differ, as scholars always do, about the truth of details. Was Isaiah of Jerusalem an aristocrat? Is Hosea's sad story based on literal truth, or is it only an allegory? They differ, too, and often widely, about material. Did Micah write or speak all of his book? Is Amos responsible for the final verses of his concluding chapter?

If we were to enter even cursorily into all these questions and arguments, we should sacrifice the portrait of each prophet, retard our narratives, shadow our pictures. This I cannot bear to do. My desire is to make each man not only real, but alive and vivid; and this desire will be thwarted by merely academic queries and quibblings.

I can only assure my readers that in every portrait drawn in the following pages I have chosen the details which seem to me the best substantiated, the most likely. The portraits are not written for the scholars, although through their learning they have supplied much of the material for them. They are, instead, written for the intelligent and, I hope, eager reader, who wants to discover through them what manner of men the great prophets really were.

I shall not, therefore, halt my sketches of them by the insertion of disagreement or argument. I shall, rather, accept the work of each prophet as we have it today in the Old

Testament (which, after all, must be the source of our further reading), realizing always that isolated verses or far longer portions may well not have been spoken or written by its reputed author. Nor shall I disrupt my narratives by any consideration of such questions as whether sycamore trees were native to the wilderness of Tekoa where Amos lived and worked. Those trees, wherever they grew, are necessary to the book of Amos, just as the donkeys which Miss Betsey Trotwood shooed off the green are necessary to *David Copperfield*. If the sycamores actually grew some miles south of Tekoa, what does it matter? Amos, as we shall see, must have been a prodigious walker!

This literary comparison to the superb novel of Dickens, a comparison which springs unbidden to my mind, does not for a moment mean that my portraits of the prophets are *fictional*. It means only that I shall do my relatively poor utmost to make each portrait as real and as true to my readers as Dickens' inimitable scenes are real to his readers, whether his donkeys were actually on the Trotwood Green or elsewhere in Dover. In other words, it means that my portraits, based as they are upon years of study both of the prophets and of their many interpreters, are written in the hope that they may afford not only interest and enlightenment, but also that excitement and even drama which are inseparable from the life of every prophet, whether from Tekoa or from Babylon. It is, in every case, the given prophet whom we want to visualize and to understand. We shall, then, not be concerned in our portraits with the insertion of scholarly theories or conclusions (unless such insertion is necessary, as it sometimes is, for the completion of our pictures), but only with the men themselves, whom I shall try to present as accurately and as truly as I can.

1

Amos

AMOS ONLY, among all the great prophets, was a man
of the desert, the desert in his case being that arid
wilderness about the region of the Dead Sea. That fact in
itself explains to a large extent his austerity, his ruthlessness,
his facing of hard facts precisely as they were, his merciless candour. He knew the torrid desert skies, the cold desert
nights, the parching winds, sandstorms, solitude, countless
hours for thought. He was more like the nomadic desert
ancestors of his people than were the other prophets. From
them he had seemingly inherited a passion for freedom, an
almost fierce sense of independence, the value of simplicity
unencumbered by the temptations of civilization in towns
and cities.

His life, before he began to prophesy and, so far as we
know, after his prophesying was completed, was a life of
necessities and essentials, unembroidered, bare. He was a
desert shepherd, following his flocks of sheep, perhaps also
of goats, in search of sparse grass and of rare springs of
water. He makes no mention of a family. He seems, indeed,

always alone, and, like any sensitive and solitary man, one given to his own thoughts.

He tells us that he was also "a gatherer of sycamore fruit," a phrase which probably means that he pricked the clustered fruits of the sycamores so that they might ripen more quickly, become more edible. These sycamores were not like the common plane trees of Europe and America, but, instead, a kind of wild fig tree, the fruit of which was presumably used as fodder for animals, perhaps even as food for very poor people.

It is not difficult to reconstruct the life of Amos in and about Tekoa, for his book is filled with imagery familiar to him and with figures of speech based on that imagery. Lions were clearly a menace to his sheep since they frequented the desert hills and were common in the valley of the Jordan even as late as New Testament times; bears also must have been known to him; and serpents crawled about the stony places in the hot sunlight. Drought and the invasions of locusts presented their problems. Since the ancient village of Tekoa, some five miles south of Bethlehem and about ten miles south of Jerusalem, marked the dividing line between the desert to the east and the fertile region of the Hebron hills to the west, he knew also the life of the farmers: the sheaves which they brought homeward in their oxen-drawn carts; the snares which they set for seed-hungry birds; the sieves which they used to shake out their corn.

He must have known earthquakes, which, in his words, made the land "rise up like a flood," even before the mighty one which took place two years before his prophetic activity and which inspired such terror and panic among the people of Israel and Judah that it was remembered and talked about hundreds of years afterward. And he may well have watched with awe a total eclipse of the sun, which, we now know, happened in the late spring of 763 B.C., probably some thirteen years before his call from God. At all events, he describes how "the earth in the clear day" had been darkened. Perhaps it was these natural wonders, these evidences of God's power and might, which contributed to his fearful understanding of Him, gave him the realization that this God was not alone the God of Israel, made him utter his stern and angry prophecies of doom and of disaster.

The visions which he relates in the familiar first person and which, through their symbolic significance, may have prepared him for his call from God contribute also to our knowledge of his life in the desert. He saw, or dreamed of a plague of grasshoppers, which were stripping the country-side of its precious spring grass; a desert fire which was devouring the land; a plumb-line by which a wall was being measured, perhaps by some farmer; a basket of fruit in the very name of which he saw destruction. These visions both in their content and in their revelations bring his life and his mind into sharp relief against their sombre background.

Amos was a Judean, a native of the southern kingdom of Judah. He prophesied in the north, in Samaria, Gilgal, and Bethel, probably at first because they offered him markets for his wool and later because upon his journeys to these towns he became constantly more aware of their perilous wealth and consequent wickedness. We know nothing whatever of his training or of where he may have received his amazing power over words, for he is one of the great literary artists of the Old Testament. Perhaps this power came only from an innate, natural eloquence, fostered as it often is by a life of loneliness and contemplation. It is impossible not to imagine him composing his furious addresses and oracles as he followed his flocks or rested among them as they cropped the scanty grass of the hills and plains.

He was as contemptuous and indignant toward individuals as he was toward the populace of the northern kingdom. His sharp retort to Amaziah, the priest at the ancient shrine of Bethel, bristles with scorn, indignation, and fury. Quite apparently he had been speaking often at Bethel before Amaziah, his patience completely exhausted, sent word to Jeroboam, the king, that Israel was no longer able to bear such words—words which included alas! the prophecy not only of Jeroboam's death, but of the eventual captivity of his nation. Amaziah's epithet of "seer," which he hurls at Amos, is clearly interpreted by Amos as an insult, since it suggests both that he has been trained in some prophetic guild and also that he may well be looking for money in exchange for silence or for return to his own land of Judah, a return which Amaziah angrily commands of him. His words to the outraged priest are as outspoken as they are relentless:

I was no prophet, neither was I a prophet's son; but I was a herdman, and a gatherer of sycamore fruit.

And the Lord took me as I followed the flock, and the Lord said unto me, Go, prophesy unto my people Israel.

Now therefore hear the word of the Lord: Thou sayest, Prophesy not against Israel, and drop not thy word against the house of Isaac.

Therefore, thus saith the Lord: Thy wife shall be a harlot in the city, and thy sons and thy daughters shall fall by the sword, and thy land shall be divided by line;

*and thou shalt die in a polluted land; and Israel shall surely
go into captivity.*

More than any other prophet Amos is both distressed and
infuriated by the injustice which he sees on every side. Idolatry he sees, too, the intrusion of sensual Canaanite practices; and he deplores it with bitter scorn. He hurls more
scorn and fury upon the false and arrogant piety in which
the people of Israel mistake the punctilious and conventional
observance of empty ceremonial for honest worship. This,
too, is idolatry, even blasphemy, and despicable in the sight
of God. Nevertheless, it is moral wrong which to Amos
is the most unforgivable of sins and against which he cries
out his most awful threats. The rich of Israel are exploiting
the poor for the miserable price of a pair of sandals; they
are spending ill-gotten gains for luxury and for splendour,
for the building of great estates, for winter homes and for
summer homes. Men and women alike drink "wine in
bowls," anoint themselves with choicest ointments, recline
on couches at meals, dance and sing, sleep upon beds of
ivory. All are regardless of the human suffering about them,
suffering which they themselves have caused by their greed
and dishonesty. They have forgotten the mercies of God in
the past history of their people, put from their minds the
vows once made to Him; therefore, punishment must be
their sure and certain reward. They shall become, cries
Amos, only like those bits which the shepherd takes out
of the mouth of a dead lion, "two legs or a piece of an ear,"
when the Lord has wreaked His righteous judgment upon
them.

Amos is also distinctive among the prophets for his recognition of the sins of neighbouring peoples, of Syria, of the
Philistines, of Phoenicia, Edom, and Moab. Not alone Israel,

but they also are children of God who have deliberately sinned against Him. At the close of his angry, courageous book he warns Israel that she is not alone in receiving God's care and protection. In His sight she is, or has become through her sins, of no more value than are the black people of Ethiopia, or than her enemies, the Philistines, whom He also led from Crete, or than the hated Syrians, whom once He guided from *their* earlier home. In such words as these, unusual, even extraordinary for his day, he not only reveals a belief in God as the Lord of all nations, but he also surely suggests that God has used in the past, and will in the future not hesitate to make use of, the enemies of Israel to bring about her irrevocable punishment.

Among all the prophets Amos is a master of climax and of irony in both his prose and his poetry. In the opening addresses of his book he vividly reveals this power of climax in his descriptions of the sins of nearby peoples, descriptions which the complacent men and women of Israel may at first have enjoyed until the prophet reaches in his mounting anger the sins of Israel and Judah, sins the most heinous of all because they of all peoples have been most blessed by God. They receive the final and most awful curses because they have not walked "after the way" of their forefathers.

Bitter questions convey his irony. *Can two walk together unless they be agreed?* he cries, meaning that God and Israel are no longer companions. *Will a lion roar in the forest when he hath no prey? Shall a trumpet be blown in the city, and the people be not afraid? Shall not the day of the Lord be darkness and not light? Even very dark, and no brightness in it?*

There is the same stinging irony in his lines of poetry,
which he utters in the words of an angry, implacable God:

I hate, I despise your feast days,
And I will not smell in your solemn assemblies.
Though ye offer me burnt offerings, I will not accept them;
Neither will I regard the peace offerings of your fat beasts.
Take away from me the noise of thy songs;
For I will not hear the melody of thy viols.
But let judgment run down as waters,
And righteousness as a mighty stream.

Amos is perhaps not an appealing prophet; he is too violent
to attract affection, and doubtless in his own day was hated
and mocked as some meddlesome madman from the desert,
who with his sinister words was interfering with the pleasant
and prosperous ways of an easy-going people. Yet he was,
and is still a mighty and towering figure in his austerity,
dignity, and righteous anger. He saw no hope for Israel,
and utters none, although even in his rage he can weep over
her as he does in the tragic and beautiful simplicity of his
little elegy in chapter 5:

The virgin of Israel is fallen.
She shall no more rise.
She is forsaken upon her land.
There is none to raise her up.

The final verses of his desperate book, verses 9 to 15,
were clearly not written by him. They are completely foreign, even contradictory to him in both language and content. They were surely added by some more hopeful disciple or, perhaps years later, by an obviously depressed

editor or compiler, who apparently could not face the un-
mitigated gloom of his words, his prophecy of doom and
utter darkness. Amos himself closed his oracles against Israel
with his rare understanding of God's fatherhood of all
people, regardless of colour or of race, and with his final,
reiterated prophecy of inescapable destruction and death.

First among the great prophets, his fearlessness, independence, and integrity must have lent courage to those
who followed him; for they surely knew of him in so small
a land, divided though it was. Isaiah of Jerusalem was his
fellow Judean. Did his own genius in irony owe perhaps
something to that of Amos? It is quite possible that as a
young man he had heard Amos speak, though such a pleasant
thought can be only conjecture.

No follower of Amos until two centuries later emphasized
and enlarged his vision of God as the Lord of all peoples,
merciful to all, yet unyielding to all in His demands for
righteousness. That was his own unique and greatest gift
to early Hebrew prophecy; and that in itself illuminates
in no small way his dark conviction of doom and of disaster.

2

Hosea

HOSEA, BOTH as man and prophet, was as hopeful and forbearing as Amos was dark and austere. This does not mean that he was not forthright and at times even harsh in his addresses to Israel, that he did not look with abhorrence upon her sins. It means only that there is an unmistakable compassion in his attitude just as there are in his speech the broken tones of one deeply moved by sorrow.

Unlike Amos, he has little to say about the other nations of his time except to warn Israel against alliances with the most powerful of them: with Egypt, always eager for the produce of Israel and Judah, especially for their oil, since Egypt grew no olive trees; with Assyria, which was growing strong under able rulers and preparing for conquest. As to smaller, closely neighbouring peoples, they are seemingly not in Hosea's mind. Surely he was not in any sense world-wide in his outlook as was Amos. To him, Israel, whom he often calls "Ephraim" with seeming affection, is God's special people, whom He loves and yearns over; and Israel,

77

to Hosea, means always the northern kingdom.

This devotion to the northern kingdom was natural to Hosea, for he was a native of Israel. Where he lived or what was his occupation, we do not know. Probably he lived in some northern town; his book, on the whole, does not suggest village life; and even though he may well not have been a farmer, he knew a great deal about the country. Perhaps he walked there to escape from his disordered home. Perhaps he took his oddly-named children with him to get them away from turmoil and confusion. It is clear that he observed the skies, their clouds, the doves and the eagles, the foam upon the swollen streams after the rains, the dew upon the fields, just as he watched the bakers at their ovens, the craftsmen melting heathen images into shape, the builders working upon their temples to foreign gods. All these sights and sounds supplied him with apt comparisons and with other figures of speech.

Hosea prophesied some few years after Amos, perhaps beginning before the death of King Jeroboam around 745 B.C. and continuing during the brief, troubled reigns of his weak successors. Several such worthless kings, following the orderly, if depraved government of Jeroboam, had made the situation in Israel even more perilous than it was in the days of Amos. Conditions, however, must have been substantially the same. Hosea, too, saw the luxury of the rich and the oppression of the poor; and in his addresses he denounces both, though never with the defiant bitterness of Amos. He saw also and cried out against adultery and licentiousness, against moral corruption of every sort. Yet what shocked him most was the idolatry of Israel, her adoration of images; the inroads upon her of Canaanite worship; the revelry at pagan festivals; the crass sexual in-

dulgences in the name of religion; the setting up of foreign
idols even in temples sacred to God Himself.

To curse such idolatry Hosea made use of a daring symbol, based upon his own unhappy marriage, a marriage
which he interprets as a strange command from God. He
describes this command, or *call*, in the first three chapters
of his book: two chapters written in the third person as
though he were relating the harrowing, disillusioning experience of another man, the third in the first person. God,
he says, has commanded him to take as his wife an adulterous
woman, a prostitute, perhaps even one of the so-called
"sacred prostitutes" attached to a Canaanite sanctuary where
she has been used by men in the fertility rites common to
such Canaanite shrines. And when, after his marriage, his
wife deserts him to return either to the lovers she has known
or to her horrible profession under the false name of religion, he "buys her back," as he is further commanded
by God to do, and again takes her into his home. By such
a marriage Hosea is convinced that he is to impress upon
Israel the realization that she, too, is a prostitute from God,
a faithless wife to Him who loves her. Hosea's own sufferings he sees as a sacrifice made to God for the sake of God's
message to Israel.

The name of this woman he gives as Gomer. She has three
children by Hosea, and their names, also commanded by
God in Hosea's story, are likewise made symbols of Israel's
impending destruction. A son is named Jezreel; and by
this name Hosea prophesies the fall of the royal house to
which King Jeroboam belongs. A daughter is named Lo-
ruhamah, which in Hebrew means *the unpitied one;* and a
second son becomes Lo-ammi, or *not my people,* which
holds the certain suggestion that the early Covenant be-

tween God and Israel is now broken because of Israel's faithlessness.

This symbolic use of a divine marriage between God and Israel was original with Hosea among the prophets, although Jeremiah, who owed much to Hosea both in material and in expression, was later to echo it in equally sad words. It could not, however, have been an entirely new thought to the wayward, idolatrous people of Israel; for the idea of a god's marriage to the land and its increase lay at the very heart of the ancient fertility cults of Canaan. Its use, then, as a metaphor was not only powerful and daring, but revealing in its new interpretation. Israel understood harlotry, both sacred and secular; and this idea of her own faithlessness to God, who had chosen her for intimate companionship and communion with Him, as Hosea again and again repeated it in his oracles and addresses, must have brought shame and humiliation to those who listened. For they had degraded God in their minds to the level of the Canaanite Baals, and even taken over into their worship of Him the rites performed in the Canaanite "high places," before rustic altars, under "sacred" trees, and in their temples.

In order to bring acutely home to Israel this faithlessness Hosea often uses the term *knowledge* of God. The word clearly means to him not only knowledge in the common conception of intelligent understanding, but also in its Old Testament meaning of intimacy. He even extends its meaning to include that intimacy by which repeatedly in Old Testament story a man *knows* a woman in the marital sense. To Hosea to *know* God is not merely a matter of right thinking or even of right worship. It is rather a matter of tender and intimate communion with Him which must result, as in human devotion at its best, in steadfast love and faithfulness. *My people are destroyed for lack of knowledge*, God says in Hosea's words. *Because thou hast rejected knowledge, I will also reject thee.*

Like the faithless Gomer, who is blind to Hosea's care, Israel does not any longer *know* that God *gave her corn and wine and oil and multiplied her silver and gold.* Nor does she *know* that in return he desires only *love and not sacrifice, the knowledge of God more than burnt offerings.*

Hosea adds to his metaphor of a marriage relationship between God and Israel the relationship between father and son. Some of his most beautiful passages stress in poetry this close kinship. In these broken rhythms one easily detects his own sad heart, his inability to be relentless and unforgiving. And here, too, is his idea of *knowledge* as the intimate understanding of God as a father and of His all-encompassing love:

> *When Israel was a child, then I loved him,*
> *And called my son out of Egypt.*
> *I taught Ephraim also to go,*
> *Taking them by their arms;*
> *But they knew not that I healed them.*
>
> *How shall I give thee up, Ephraim?*
> *How shall I deliver thee, Israel?*

To this second of the prophets, then, these comparisons to intimate human relationships describe most clearly God's love for men. To Israel, He is both husband and father; to Him, Israel is both wife and child. And it is precisely this personal imagery which lends to Hosea's book its almost overwhelming tenderness and compassion.

He inveighs, it is true, against the seeking of foreign
alliances, seeing only folly and stupidity in Israel's slavish
overtures to Egypt and to Assyria, who want only to devour
her. He cries out against her idolatries, her worship of the
molten bulls of Samaria, which supposedly represent God,
but which are made only by ignorant "workmen." Like
Amos he is sure of deserved retribution and awful punishment, which he describes like the deadly attack of a lion,
or like the slow corruption of moth and rot, or like some
sudden and devastating natural disaster. Nevertheless, his
disorderly, broken verses, which more than anything else
resemble the anxious, distraught, pitying accents of an
anguished human voice, are never entirely divorced from
this tender and intimate concern of God, this love for His
people in spite of their sins against Him.

Hosea's book is not an easy one to read, largely because
of its swift changes of mood in which threatening gives
way to hope, curses to blessings, disgust and hatred to love.
In order to read it intelligently and, therefore, to understand its author, one should be aware of its three parts: the
first, a biographical and autobiographical account of Hosea's
marriage, given in chapters 1 to 3; the second, a series of
addresses, probably, in the form we now have them, much
mutilated from a lost original (if there were, indeed, a complete original) and given in chapters 4 to 11; and, lastly,
a final chapter, 14, in which Hosea expresses both hope and
expectation of the return of Israel to God and of her re-
instatement as His people.

In this final brief chapter of his book Hosea seemingly
gathers together all his indictments against Israel, all God's
fears for her: her idols and her images; her dependence upon
nations which will but turn and rend her; her faithlessness;

her harlotry; her seeming disregard of the swift horses of Assyria. Yet he gathers also all his hopes, all the mercies of God, whose anger must at last give way before His love. Hosea sees in this conclusion the beauty of Israel at last renewed and flourishing like the olive trees upon her hillsides or the cedars of Lebanon, like the growing corn and the vine or a green fir tree, which are all still, as they were in the past, the gifts of God.

Like Amos, although in a totally different way, Hosea speaks with eloquence and power. His eloquence does not lie in terse, carefully knit sentences, in mounting climax or in sharp, almost cruel irony, but rather in a peculiarly moving cadence, in the rise and fall of reproofs, questions, pleadings. As Amos can see only doom and destruction, so Hosea, although he sees and fears both, can never entirely relinquish hope.

He is the prophet of the sufferers, of those who bear unreasonable, unexplainable sorrows to which there are no answers. Since he, with Jeremiah, was the most human of all the prophets, he must often have questioned his strange assignment from God, even although in his incredible faith he believed that he knew the answer, understood the price he must pay in return for God's actual need of him.

3

Isaiah of Jerusalem

ISAIAH OF Jerusalem was a very different man from the
two prophets in the northern kingdom and from his
Judean contemporary, Micah. Although he was distressed
by the situations which they deplored, by injustice committed by men of wealth and power, by idolatry and licentiousness, by the oppression of the poor, and although he
cried out vehemently against these wrongs, he was, nevertheless, in contrast to his fellow prophets, a conservative,
a well-to-do man of culture and sophistication, one who
knew kings as companions, one who, in spite of its obvious
sins, looked upon the reigning House of David in the kingdom of Judah with affection and respect, perhaps even with
a measure of veneration. Unlike them all, too, he was an adviser in political affairs, not improbably a king's councillor.
The state as an institution deeply concerned him; and he
was clearly interested in international as well as in national
questions and problems. Some scholars think he may have
been a priest, or at least trained as one; for he was surely a
man of education, no shepherd or small farmer, but instead,

85

a gentleman of learning, of urbanity, and of social standing in Jerusalem. His various uses of language, the ease and marked skill of his writing, prove in themselves his sophistication and cosmopolitanism.

He was always a man of the city. He loved Jerusalem, which had once been "faithful": its narrow, crowded streets, its Temple on its hill, its pool and stream of Shiloah, the waters of which "go softly." He quite clearly was familiar with the upper circles of its society, with judges, priests, counsellors, and even kings. He knew its women, their vanities, their love of adornment, their beautiful clothing, all of which stood him in good stead in his bitter satires on their absurd pride and complacency. Yet he knew also the country beyond the city gates, its vineyards, its gardens, its farm animals. His very love for Jerusalem, his innate respect for her institutions, his association with her men of power, lend added courage to his denunciations against her. His patriotism for his city seemingly endured; yet it never deluded him as to the consequences of her stupidity and her sin.

His prophetic ministry was longer than that of any prophet of his time and probably the most influential. According to his own account, he began to prophesy upon the death of King Uzziah of Judah, probably around 740–742 B.C.; and he was still active forty years later when Sennacherib of Assyria besieged Jerusalem in 701 B.C. after some years of ravaging Judea. There may well have been a long interim in his ministry when, about 734 B.C., King Ahaz refused to accept his urging not to make dangerous alliances either with neighbouring peoples or with foreign powers. Very probably during this interim he himself recorded his vision and call from God and his frustrating experience with King Ahaz, together with certain of his early oracles. He surely suggests this recording in chapter 8 of his long book. That he was vastly able both to write his oracles and to describe his experiences is certain in view of his background—a certainty not so easy to assume of Amos, Hosea, and Micah.

The book of Isaiah is perhaps the most untidy and disorderly among all books of the Old Testament. Scholars have worked upon it for many years; yet not one is able to give confident assurance either of the exact dates of its manifold contents or of the identity of all its many authors. They venture only to say that the actual and best work of Isaiah of Jerusalem is without much doubt contained in its first twelve chapters; that other work of his is probably written in chapters 28 to 31; and that all of his prophecy, intermingled as it is with other material, concludes with chapter 39, perhaps better with chapter 33, since chapters 34 and 35 clearly belong elsewhere and chapters 36 to 39 are chapters of biography, which are much the same as chapters 18 to 20 in the book of II Kings and probably taken from that historical book.

Yet there are twenty-seven more chapters in this prodigious book called *Isaiah*. What about them? Why were they attached to the writings of Isaiah of Jerusalem with whom they have clearly nothing to do? These questions are among the most baffling in the entire Old Testament. Perhaps, several realistic scholars have suggested, some ancient scribe, who made the first copy of this motley, unrelated material, wanted to save the expensive parchment upon which he was writing and, because of his thrift, continued with chapter 40 in order not to waste the clean remainder of his scroll. He was neither an historian nor a literary artist. He had merely been set to copying as accurately and carefully as he could a mass of material which learned Hebrew compilers and editors had decided must be preserved. Who wrote what, and when, were not *his* concern!

Through the careful researches of scholars, however, and the personal affirmations of Isaiah of Jerusalem, we now know beyond the shadow of any doubt that chapters 6, 7, and 8 were written by him, just as we know that chapters 40 to 55, with the preceding 34 and 35, were *not* written by him, but, rather, nearly two hundred years later by a poet whom we call Isaiah of Babylon, or Second Isaiah. We know also that chapters 56 to 66 must have been written by some other unknown poet, whom we call the Third Isaiah, since they obviously describe a still later time after the exiles in Babylon had come back home to a disrupted and disappointing land. So, in this book of Isaiah, we have really *three* books; and, within each of the three, other passages and often entire chapters written by no "Isaiah" at all, but by men whose names have been lost for centuries, if, indeed, they were ever known.

Such conclusions as these serve to show how difficult and disarranged is this long Old Testament book, which, nevertheless, contains perhaps the most beautiful and inspiriting literary work of the entire Bible. As intelligent readers, however, we must take things as they are, not as we might wish them to be, and study this greatest of all the eighth century prophets, Isaiah of Jerusalem, through those portions of his book which we can safely assume to be his own.

We can take pleasure and assurance, too, in the knowledge that the book of Isaiah as we now have it in the Old

Testament is substantially identical with its earliest known manuscript. This encouraging, even thrilling fact was not made clear until some fifteen years ago. Until the spring of the year 1947 there was in existence no *complete* manuscript of the Hebrew text of Isaiah earlier than around 1000 A.D., seventeen hundred years after Isaiah of Jerusalem recorded his dramatic call, his talks with King Ahaz of Judah, his oracles and addresses, and at least twelve hundred years after they were collected and edited by Hebrew scholars.

But by 1948 this ancient Hebrew prophet had made the headlines of all the best newspapers throughout the civilized world! For in the spring of 1947, in a cave on a precipitous cliff overlooking the western shore of the Dead Sea, some scrolls were discovered by Bedouin boys in search of a stray goat, rolls of parchment in stone jars which proved to be manuscripts of great age and importance. One of these manuscripts, the most prized, was a complete *Isaiah*, which, when studied by the best Hebrew scholars, was dated by the great majority of them in either the first century B.C. or perhaps even in the second—in other words, not far from its original publication around 200 B.C.

There can be few, if any readers of this book of mine who do not know of this exciting first discovery, of more caves and of their treasures, and of the ancient monastery at Qumran, now excavated, where these so-called Dead Sea Scrolls were copied during those distant years of the last centuries before Christ and the earliest centuries of the Christian era. The book of Isaiah must have been a favourite among those brethren of that Jewish sect known as the Essenes who lived and copied at Qumran; for several fragments and incomplete manuscripts of it have since been found in other eagerly explored caves. And most exciting, and significant of all information which the caves have yielded, is the fact that this earliest of all known *Isaiahs* is, except for a few unimportant particulars, practically identical with the earliest Hebrew text heretofore in existence, the text upon which our own Old Testament book is based. In other words, the Dead Sea Scroll of *Isaiah* shows the same composite material, the same copying of the work of Isaiah of Babylon, and of the so-called Third Isaiah, the same inclusion of the oracles of other unknown authors.

The utterances of Isaiah of Jerusalem, then, have always been difficult to determine, to extricate with entire confidence from the mass of prose and poetry which around 200 B.C. was issued under his name by the Hebrew scholars assembling and editing the works of their prophets. All students of this Isaiah have known difficulties and problems, have asked their questions for many centuries. Nor have even the best scholars been able to give sure and certain answers. Still, they have done their utmost, with the result that readers of today are able to picture Isaiah of Jerusalem as a great prophetic figure; to be relatively certain of what he did and thought and said; and to recognize in him, as the Qumran copyists recognized in their rude *scriptoria* by the Dead Sea and as countless millions through succeeding centuries have recognized, one of the most faithful, most gifted, most heroic of men.

We shall be wise if we start to read his book with chapter 6. This chapter was one of the first recorded by him. If it were not the very first, it should have been; for it relates his initial encounter with God, and, at least in a literary sense, it unquestionably forms the beginning of his book. In it he describes in eloquent, exalted, and yet peculiarly simple and direct prose—prose unexcelled, if, indeed, equalled throughout the Old Testament—his amazing experience in the Temple at Jerusalem, to which he had gone, perhaps for some great festival observance, perhaps only for personal meditation and prayer. We do not know how old he was at the time, but in view of the many years of his ministry, we can safely picture him as a young man, probably in his early twenties.

This greatest single experience of his life constituted his *call* from God, a call surely never forgotten by him in its every dramatic detail: the actual vision of God Himself, "the Lord, high and lifted up"; the six-winged seraphim, themselves so overcome by the Holy Presence that they cover their faces with their wings as they cry to one another, *Holy, holy, holy is the Lord of hosts;* Isaiah's instant and sorrowful realization of his own utter unworthiness; the glowing coal from the altar with which one of the seraphim touches his lips to free him from his sense of sin; the voice of the Lord calling for someone to proclaim His message; Isaiah's immediate and eager response. He evidently then and there began his ministry to Jerusalem and Judea, which, although it may have been halted for a time, extended, as we have seen, over some forty years.

More than any other of our great prophets Isaiah of Jerusalem embraced in his teachings and his denunciations both a greater variety of subjects and a far wider and more various means of expression. He was deeply concerned with the political situation of the southern kingdom; with the menace of Assyrian imperialism; with the appalling social sins and even crimes of his people; with the inevitable near and awful future; and yet with the hope of final salvation for at least a *remnant* of Israel. His writing ranges from narratives in prose to the most exalted of poetry, such range, indeed, that a study of him as a literary artist will form a later chapter of this book. Here we shall now consider the content of his prophecies in order to see him as the amazing man he was.

We know little about his background or of his own immediate family, although we have safely inferred a good deal both from his own details and from his manner of speaking. If he were not married at the time of his vision in the Temple, he must have been shortly thereafter; for on the momentous occasion when at the command of God he met King Ahaz "at the end of the conduit of the upper pool," he took with him his son, a boy called Shear-ja-shub, a symbolic name like those of the three children of Hosea and meaning in Hebrew *a remnant shall return*. His interview with King Ahaz, who seems to have been looking into the water supply of Jerusalem in case of a siege of the city, was disappointing in the extreme. Ahaz refused to listen to his advice against any dealings with the neighbouring kingdoms of Syria and Israel, which ostensibly wanted support against Assyria, but which were really conspiring against Ahaz himself.

To Ahaz, a practical politician, Isaiah was an absurd visionary, an unrealistic idealist, with his counsel for dependence only upon God. Years later, after Isaiah's silence during the reign of Ahaz, he was to give King Hezekiah, the son of Ahaz and a far more religious man, the same advice, now against overtures to Egypt for help against the more imminent threat of Assyria, which had already ravaged the northern kingdom. Such overtures to Egypt, to her horses and chariots, meant to Isaiah "a covenant with death." Hezekiah was to see forty and more of his towns and cities destroyed, Egypt beaten, and himself shut up in Jerusalem "like a bird in a cage," under which hopeless prospect he was forced to submit and to pay tribute to the Assyrian king, Sennacherib, in order that Jerusalem should escape ravaging and pillage.

To Isaiah, Assyria is the "rod of God's anger." There is no escape from the desolation she will make of Judea, the cities she will burn, the land she will devour. Jerusalem, although she may escape for a season, will eventually become like some deserted cottage overgrown with vines, like a garden that has no water. In order to emphasize this sure and certain fate to the apostate and faithless people of his city and his country, Isaiah named his second son Maher-shalal-hash-baz, which means *the spoiler cometh quickly, the plundering is swift*. God, always the God of history to Isaiah of Jerusalem as to the other prophets, is surely using Assyria to wreak His righteous vengeance; and yet he makes clear that her turn for punishment is coming. The Assyrians, too, he warns, shall fall by the sword, and by the sword of no mean nation.

Like Amos, Isaiah denounces the moral corruption of his people. They are "a sinful nation," one "laden with iniquity," filled with "wounds and bruises and putrifying sores." God hates their oppression of the poor just as He is "weary" of their "vain oblations," their incense, their observance of "new moons," their solemn, yet empty assemblies; for their "hands are full of blood." Jerusalem has become a harlot. Once the home of righteousness, it is now the home of murderers, of rebellious princes, the companions of thieves. The stupid, vain women of Jerusalem, who flaunt their rings and nose jewels, their mirrors and their well-set hair, will see the day when so many of their husbands are killed in war that seven of them will beg marriage of one man. They will gladly buy their own bread and their own clothing, they will tell him, if only he will lend them his name to take away their humiliation and disgrace!

It is the sin of pride to which Isaiah of Jerusalem again and again returns in his scornful outbursts; and he constantly sees this pride in the imagery of height, of pretentious arrogance. He compares the loftiness and the haughtiness of men and women to the high cedars of Lebanon and the great oaks of Bashan, to the height of the mountains, even to that of walls and towers made by human hands. Only the Lord of hosts is to be exalted. All proud men must be brought low. The worst vice of Assyria, too, is her pride, the "high looks" of her king, the overbearing arrogance of her horses and her chariots. When the Lord is finished with Assyria's punishment of Israel and Judah, He will bring down her own pride even to the dust.

Imagery such as this, the constant employment of sights familiar to his hearers, marks Isaiah of Jerusalem as an actor; and an actor he surely was both in speech and behaviour. He did more than choose strange names for his sons, who must have been called something more simple in the family circle, by their puzzled mother, and by their friends. If he did not walk "barefoot and naked" through the Jerusalem streets to symbolize the final fate of his people, one can easily imagine his doing so. If he did not play on a harp when he went about singing his song of God's vineyard, it was an act most characteristic of him. Drama was inherent in him. All his vivid and startling words proclaim his dramatic sense of language, in which he was more skillful and dexterous than was any other prophet.

Yet, with all his assurance of doom and desolation, this prophet of Jerusalem is never devoid of hope. From the beginning of his ministry, through the name given to his older son, he insisted that a *remnant* must return. What did he mean by this remnant? In the early days of his prophesying he may have meant the ruling House of Judah, the dynasty of David, which some wise and righteous prince might at last redeem. Later, as he saw certain destruction drawing nearer, he perhaps meant his disciples, honourable men whom he had apparently drawn about him and who embodied his own hopes. At the last, when Judea had become a tribute-paying state to Assyria, he still clung to his faith that somehow, perhaps far in the future, the way to Jerusalem would become a highway for the remnant of God's people "which shall be left from Assyria; like as it was to Israel in the day that he came up out of the land of Egypt."

Nothing is known about Isaiah of Jerusalem after the Assyrian siege of Judea and the temporary survival of his capital city. He seems to have concluded his prophetic ministry around 701 B.C., although we cannot be certain of exact dates. Nor can we be at all sure that he looked ahead more than a century and saw the rise of Babylon, which was not only to conquer Assyria but to lead Jerusalem and Judea into captivity. The verses of chapter 39 which describe this prophecy were taken, as we have seen, from the book of II Kings and may well refer to events long after his day. The charming story in chapter 38 of this extracted biography, a story which recounts his curing King Hezekiah's boil with a poultice of figs, is probably more apocryphal than actual; and there is no substantiated truth in the Jewish legend that he was martyred under the cruel

and wicked Manasseh, the son of Hezekiah, who succeeded
his father around 687 B.C., although such a fate does not
seem unlikely.

We can surely believe that his long ministry to his people was marked at its end as at its beginning by the strength
and brilliance of his personality and by the unexcelled and
various power of his literary art. Small wonder that Dante
nearly two thousand years after his day quotes from him
in the *Paradise* of his *Divine Comedy*! Isaiah seems to have
taught Dante more than a little both about the holiness of
God and about the incomparable use of language.

4

Micah

IN WILLIAM HAZLITT'S essay "On the Pleasure of Hating," a charming essay in spite of its bitterness and disillusionment, he says: "Without something to hate, we should lose the very spring of thought and action." Perhaps Hazlitt, theological student though he was in his early life, did not know too much about Micah; yet he could not have found more apt and succinct words had he been describing the ruling motive of this prophet of Judea.

Micah was a prime hater. Hatred was, indeed, the very spring of his thought and his action. He hated cities, even Jerusalem, the capital city of his country, which as early as his day was revered as a holy city. He hated the Assyrians. He hated the rich. And, above all else, he hated the wrongs committed by men against their fellows. His brief book, more than half of which he probably did not write, or speak, flames with righteous hatred, with justified fury and condemnation.

Among all the great prophets Micah has been quite wrongly underestimated, not sufficiently appreciated or valued. Perhaps this unfortunate fact has its source in the little which is known about him. Unlike all the other prophets he says nothing about his call from God. We do not know whether, like Isaiah, his great contemporary, he had a vision, or whether God "took" him while he was labouring in his fields, as Amos was "taken" while he followed his sheep. The details of this call Micah apparently considered unimportant; the reality of it governed all his life.

He came from Moresheth, a village near the Philistine city of Gath. Today it is called Marissa, in the Arabic form of its name. This village, or small town, was situated in the southwestern part of Judea in a region known as the Shephalah, which lies in the foothills between the fertile coastal plain above the Mediterranean and the central highlands. The region is, and was even in Micah's day, a district of vineyards, olive groves, and of good farming land, upon which the shrewd and prosperous land-grabbers of Jerusalem naturally longed to place their rapacious hands.

Small though it was as a settlement, this Moresheth in Micah's time was not unimportant, since it lay in the direct line of any attack which might be made against Judea by armies advancing either from the south or from the west. It had, in fact, known such attacks from Egyptian bands two hundred years before Micah lived; and it was to know others long afterward by Roman armies, and, more than a thousand years after the Romans, by the clashing forces of the Saracens and of Christian Crusaders. Micah was clearly concerned for the peaceful welfare of his native town; for he speaks, or writes, of his haunting fear of invasion from literally any enemy upon the march.

Our best source for both the time and the importance of Micah comes from Jeremiah, who in the 26th chapter of his long book says that Micah prophesied in the years of King Hezekiah of Judah, years which probably lay between 715 and 687 B.C. Perhaps we shall not be far wrong if we place Micah, as most of the best scholars do, in the years between 714 and 700. These dates mean that he had already seen the terrible downfall of the northern kingdom before the hosts of Assyria in 722 B.C., and that in 701, just before the close of his ministry, he saw the sparing of Jerusalem by the ravaging armies of Sennacherib after they had despoiled the countryside of Judea. Micah had prophesied the ruin of Jerusalem, its being "plowed like a field." Was he disappointed that, in the face of all its wickedness, it was left standing for a brief season by the Assyrian king?

Micah was perhaps a small artisan in Moresheth, or perhaps merely a peasant farmer. Like St. Francis of Assisi, like John Wesley, he was a champion of the poor, of little, unimportant people. Did he know Isaiah of Jerusalem? To be sure, he (or some disciple of his) echoes words from Isaiah, words which describe the beating of swords into ploughshares and of spears into pruning hooks. Or did Isaiah echo Micah's words? It seems impossible to be sure which was the debtor to which, or whether both were debtors to someone else. Contemporaries as they were and both Judeans, they, one feels, must have been aware of each other. Still, there was a wide social gulf between Isaiah and Micah, a gulf not easily bridged in their class-conscious day. Most of Micah's words sound far more like those of Amos, a countryman like himself. Amos had lived only some twenty miles from Moresheth; and Micah must have known of him. Perhaps he was even familiar with the oracles of the older prophet. Who can tell?

There is something extremely disarming about Micah. Perhaps this feeling of admiration and affection for him arises from his complete honesty and simplicity, from the directness of all his words. Much as he hated cities, neither they nor their inhabitants daunted him in the least. One must gather from his addresses that he gave them in Jerusalem rather than in the country, to the heads of the rich houses, even to the princes, the priests, and to the official Temple "seers" and "prophets," who, he says, "divine for money" and even dare to "lean upon the Lord." He hurls his scornful questions upon the capital cities of both north and south:

What is the transgression of Jacob? Is it not Samaria?
And what are the high places of Judah? Are they not
    Jerusalem?

It is the rich of the cities who receive his scathing condemnation, they who "covet" the fields of the poor and "take them by violence," who cast out the country women "from their pleasant houses," who build up Jerusalem "with blood and with iniquity." Likewise, it is the cities whose gates will be stormed by Assyria and which shall become as devastated fields and desolated vineyards.

Micah is entirely selfless in his rage and indignation against the moral corruption of Jerusalem and Judah. There is no humiliation which he will not gladly undergo in order to make his country aware of her sins. That his words and his work for God were familiar to Jeremiah many years after his death is evidence of his courage and his value.

More than half of Micah's brief book was probably not written, or spoken, by him. Like the concluding verses of the book of Amos, much of chapters 4 to 7 in the book of Micah is quite unlike him. Revengeful though these chapters are in many passages, their recurring theme of ultimate salvation, of the remnant to be restored, is surely not characteristic of Micah. He was too obsessed with the sins of Jerusalem and Judah, with the terrors which lay in wait for them, to envisage their restoration and their future years of peace. In the several centuries between his prophecies and their final editing, utterances of unknown writers may well have been added to them, a custom common to the final form of other Old Testament books.

Nevertheless, those of us who admire him hate to deprive him of those verses in chapter 6, verses for centuries accredited to him. If he did not himself speak them, they embody all his values: his fierce sense of justice; his scorn of hypocrisy; his care for the simple people among whom he lived and whose devoted friend he was; his honesty and humility; his entire lack of pretension. These verses are written, too, after his manner, in swift question and direct answer. We shall probably never know whether or not he spoke them; but let us, like countless thousands of readers throughout long centuries, believe, or at least *imagine* that he did. For nothing of all which, we are sure, he did say is more like him.

Here the ironic questions are supposedly asked by his listeners, perhaps in fury at his upbraidings, perhaps also in satirical reference to pagan rites. The answer is given by the prophet in behalf of God:

Will the Lord be pleased with thousands of rams,
Or with ten thousands of rivers of oil?
Shall I give my firstborn for my transgression,
The fruit of my body for the sin of my soul?

He hath showed thee, O man, what is good:
And what doth the Lord require of thee
But to do justly, and to love mercy,
And to walk humbly with thy God?

5

Jeremiah

EXCEPT FOR David, about whom we have in the book of II Samuel a detailed and even magnificent biography together with more material in the preceding book of I Samuel, Jeremiah is probably the most fully drawn, the best known, of all figures in the Old Testament. In his long book of fifty-two chapters he tells us a great deal about himself; and his friend and secretary, Baruch, in the same book tells us more, presumably at Jeremiah's request, perhaps at his dictation.

Moreover, Jeremiah is the least reserved of any of the prophets. With the utmost candour he lets us into his heart, a word which to the ancient Hebrews meant the mind and the soul, not so much the source of affections as that of thought and inspiration. Unlike Hosea, whose work Jeremiah clearly knew and admired and whom he resembled both in personality and in his manner of writing, he leaves nothing to the imagination of his readers. Unlike Isaiah of Jerusalem, who was reserved and conservative, Jeremiah knows no reserve. Of all the prophets, except perhaps for

Hosea, he was unquestionably the most human; and even more than does Hosea, who was given to suggestion rather than to delineation, he lets us into his life.

Jeremiah had countless faults and shortcomings. He was guilty of irritation, impatience, petulance, hopelessness, doubt, complaint, fear, fury, and even of self-pity. He was at odds not only with men, but often with God. When he cried out that the heart of man "is deceitful above all things and desperately wicked," he referred to his own stubborn heart as well as to those of his tormentors. He could, and did curse his mother, who bore him, and his father, who rejoiced that he had a son. Nevertheless, with all his human frailties, he was patient, long-suffering, hopeful, bold, even heroic. He endured more than did any other prophet; he was mocked, humiliated, rejected, scorned, persecuted, even tortured. He was surely one of the loneliest of men, sacrificing marriage, children, and friends for the sake of his calling; yet, though he dares to accuse God of lying and to compare Him to a deceitful brook with no water in it, he says that without God he burns as with fire and that, although he has sworn to have nothing more to do with Him, he cannot live without speaking God's message to those who despise both God and him.

Like David, who was the most contradictory and paradoxical of men, now faithless, now consumed by faith, at once evil and good, sensitive and ruthless, and who shares with Jeremiah the distinction of being well-known both to his age and to ours, so Jeremiah was a man of contradictions, of seemingly opposite qualities: a man of despair and of faith, of resolution and indecision, of utter defeat and failure, yet of victory and triumph. No other prophet experienced so often and so deeply "dark nights of the soul";

yet not one came out of those nights so triumphantly as did Jeremiah, or saw so clearly through the darkness the dawn of a new day for his country and for his people.

He had no inclination, no desire to prophesy. He would far rather have stayed quietly in his home village of Anathoth, some three or four miles north of Jerusalem. In one of his poems he longs for "a lodging place of a wayfarer" that he might escape there far from the "treacherous men" with whom he is fated to live.

There is every evidence in his long book that he knew and loved the country. He writes of its high, snow-covered mountains, its heathland, its flowering trees, its animals, wild asses, lions, wolves, the hinds looking for grass. He had watched the farmers in their fields; he mentions even the herbs which grew there. There is more than a little suggestion that he knew a great deal about birds. He writes of the partridge, the stork, the turtle dove, the eagles, cranes, swallows, now and again describing their habits; and he uses their instinctive migrations, "the times of their coming," to contrast their sure ways with the ignorance and the indifference of the people of Judah.

He had apparently a great love for the northern kingdom of Israel, which a hundred years earlier had been destroyed by Assyria. His own tribe of Benjamin had come from the north. As they were to Hosea, the people of Israel are "Ephraim" to him; and he cannot give up hope that they may some day return home. In one of the most moving passages of his poetry he writes of "Rachel weeping for her children" and refusing to be comforted "because they were not." Rachel was, of course, the tribal mother of *all* Israel; yet in this passage the prophet pictures her as mourning over the north, over the people of Jacob, always dear to Jeremiah.

Jeremiah clearly came from well-to-do people and from a priestly family. His father, a priest, was named Hilkiah; and the family may well have descended from a long line of priests, which descent meant that Jeremiah was an educated man, as, indeed, his skillful command of language proves. That he was bitter and condemnatory toward the Jerusalem priests, his enemies, lay in the fact that they were official and professional priests, subservient to the national interests of the state and to the king and dedicated only in name to God.

He records with complete candour his *call* from God, which, in contrast to the calls of the prophets preceding him, came three times and in three quite different ways. The first call was a commandment from God, "the Lord," who told him that even before his birth God had ordained him to be a prophet. Jeremiah's response shows his sensitive and retiring nature, even his timidity; for, unlike Isaiah, who a hundred years earlier had accepted eagerly and at once, he says that he cannot speak, for he is but "a child." God, however, is relentless. To further His demands of Jeremiah He shows him a flowering almond tree, which in Hebrew means the *awakener* or the *watcher*. Again, He makes Jeremiah see a boiling pot, which faces toward the north and which to the prophet is a symbol of invasion, terror, and destruction.

Jeremiah, again unlike Isaiah, is never entirely convinced that God can make of him "an iron pillar" or "a brazen wall." He accepts the call, always an unwanted task, only because of God's promise to be with him "against the kings of Judah, against the princes, against the priests, and against the people of the land," because he knows beyond any shadow of doubt that God is shaping the history of his time, and because he can see no honourable way out for a lover of his nation and for a servant of God.

Although he was surely not recognized as such in his time, Jeremiah was actually the outstanding figure of his age and, as we have already learned, one of the dominant figures of Old Testament history. To the people of his day, especially to the ruling classes of Judah, to her priests and her official prophets, he was without doubt a thorn in the flesh, a fanatic, and even the maddest of men. During his early years as a prophet they resented him bitterly as a crass interferer in the affairs of an outwardly prosperous nation; during his later years, when Babylon was threatening conquest and destruction, they hated and feared him as a stubborn and ceaseless harbinger of disaster.

Jeremiah's time was one of impending darkness and chaos. If we accept his own statement at the beginning of his book, he began to preach and to prophesy around 626 B.C. "in the thirteenth year" of the reign of King Josiah, who ruled the kingdom of Judah probably from 640 until 609 B.C. Some scholars question this date, 626 B.C., on the ground that the writings of both Jeremiah and Baruch describe the events of later times; yet more trust to Jeremiah's own words, even though most of his writings may well have been done during the later years of his ministry, that is, after the death of King Josiah. Perhaps they were written, or re-written, during the time when Jeremiah was obliged to go into hiding after his life was threatened by King Jehoiakim.

Jeremiah knew well three kings of Judah during his long life of work for his stricken country: King Josiah, whom he at first honoured for his attempts at reform; King Jehoiakim, whom he scorned and despised for his violence and

oppression; and King Zedekiah, placed on the throne by
Nebuchadnezzar of Babylon during the last years of Judah
as a kingdom, from 598 to 587 B.C. Like Isaiah, Jeremiah
seems to have been on intimate terms with these rulers,
though his counsels, like those of Isaiah, were usually treated
with contempt and scorn. Josiah, often known as the "re-
forming king," did his utmost to do away with the heathen
practices of his forerunner Manasseh, the worship even in
the Temple at Jerusalem of Assyrian deities, the human sacrifices allowed and even encouraged by Manasseh. These
reforms, however, proved in the end hollow and meaningless to Jeremiah, since he saw that they were largely external,
that they dealt with Temple ordinances rather than with
the inner spirit and moral behaviour of the people of Judah.
The prophet knew only too well the brutality of King
Jehoiakim, who upon one occasion cut in pieces and burned
in a brazier Jeremiah's condemnatory scrolls against the
idolatry of Jerusalem and Judah. He lived to see the last
king of Judah, Zedekiah, blinded by Nebuchadnezzar and
taken in chains to Babylon.

Like Isaiah, Jeremiah protested against alliances with foreign powers. He saw only calamity from Egypt, now ready
to throw in her lot with Assyria against the rising power of
Babylon, a calamity only too well realized in the death of
Josiah at Egyptian hands. He saw, too, the utter uselessness
of any revolt of the small neighbouring peoples of Judah
against the great powers either of Egypt or of Babylon. In
612 B.C. he saw the destruction of Nineveh, the Assyrian
capital, "that bloody city," whose "lies and robberies" the
poet and prophet Nahum had so brilliantly described in his
brief book; and from then on he became convinced that the
conquest of Judah by Babylon was inevitable, indeed the

vengeance of God against the wickedness of His people. Traitor though he was called by the ruling classes of Judah, befriended by but a few men, beaten and imprisoned, he nevertheless persisted in his conviction; and this conviction was realized when the forces of Nebuchadnezzar, who was infuriated by the senseless revolt of King Zedekiah, probably in league with Egypt, carried away the leading people of Jerusalem after a final siege and destruction of the city in 587 B.C.

We know nothing of Jeremiah's death. It probably took place in Egypt where he was apparently forced to flee by his terrified countrymen. Tradition says that he was stoned to death there by exasperated and angry Judeans, whom he continued to rebuke for their cowardice and folly. If we can trust the 44th chapter of his book, he lived for some ten years in Egypt, still protesting, still mocked and hated.

It is probably unwise, however, to place too much faith in the literal truth of the final chapters of Jeremiah's book, rich and brilliant as it is in its portraiture both of himself and of his age. As a book, it is even more difficult to read in its present form than is that of Isaiah, largely because its wealth of material lacks chronological order. Yet its chapters, although most of them cannot be exactly dated in terms of the time of their writing, reveal unmistakably the nature of the writer: his confessions alike of despair and of faith; the wrongs against which he is boldly crying out; his convictions of the purposes of God even in the midst of his personal humiliation and suffering; and his undying faith in the future of both Judah and Israel. Through these four contributions to Old Testament prophecy we are able to see what manner of man he was and what he gave, sometimes unwillingly but always bravely, not only to his own desperate times, but to ages yet to come.

Like St. Augustine nearly a thousand years after Jeremiah's day, Jeremiah, too, wrote Confessions, although unlike Augustine he does not seem to have written them for publication. They seem rather to be pages from a personal journal, or diary, inmost thoughts written down perhaps in an attempt to free the prophet's soul from doubt and anguish. It is possible that they were gathered together by Baruch, who would surely have perceived their value both as literature and as a revelation of character; but of the source of their survival we can have no sure knowledge. They are written largely in poetry, and, together with the story of Jeremiah's call are contained, along with much unrelated material, in the first twenty chapters of his book.

These *Confessions* are of incomparable value to our understanding of Jeremiah, for such personal and intimate revelations are not so fully given elsewhere in the Old Testament, except in the book of Job and in the Psalms, upon which latter book Jeremiah's confessions are thought to have had great influence. They are, in a very real sense, poems of mood, of protest, of inner turmoil, doubt, anger, questioning; and questioning not only of Jeremiah's fate, but concerning the mystery of life, the unanswerable problem of human sorrow. Certain of them are composed in the form of poetic dialogue between Jeremiah and God:

Jeremiah asks:

Wherefore doth the way of the wicked prosper?
Wherefore are all they happy that deal treacherously?

God answers, or rather does not answer, but replies with His own question:

If thou hast run with the footmen and they have wearied
  thee,
Then how canst thou contend with horses?

Jeremiah speaks again:

I sat not in the assembly of the mockers,
I sat alone because of thy hand.
For thou hast filled me with indignation.

And God says:

If thou return, then will I bring thee again,
And thou shalt stand before me.

And I will deliver thee out of the hand of the wicked,
And I will redeem thee out of the hand of the terrible.

As Hosea had seen the northern kingdom a hundred years
earlier as a harlot, the faithless wife of God, who had brought
her forefathers up from Egyptian bondage and made a
Covenant with them, so Jeremiah in the same image sees his
southern kingdom of Judah. Standing in the gate of the
Temple, which in his words has become "a den of robbers,"
he accuses the men of Jerusalem and Judah of walking after
strange gods, of committing adultery, of shedding inno-
cent blood. He berates the women for making cakes to
offer to the heathen "queen of heaven," and even the children for gathering wood for their mothers' fires. He does
not need to cry that he is filled with "the fury of the Lord,"
that he is weary with holding that fury in check, for nothing could be more evident.
With unparalleled violence and awful concreteness of

language, with fierce abandon unknown to any other prophet, he tells rulers, priests, court prophets, and people that they are brutish corrupters, false dealers, licentious slanderers, abominations in the sight of God. He swears that their carcasses shall be as dung upon the fields, meat for vultures, devoured by beasts. He declares that death is already at their windows and that there will be none to bury them. He draws a terrifying picture of the ghastly silence which shall fall upon Jerusalem: no sound of mirth in her streets, no voice of gladness either of bride or of bridegroom. The few that are left of this "evil family" shall long for death rather than for life; but to these even death shall be denied. For the men of Judah and the dwellers in Jerusalem, saith the Lord, have broken the Covenant which He formed with their fathers and have caused Him to be a stranger in the land, to be like "a wayfaring man," who can find not so much as a lodging for the night.

As Assyria to Isaiah was the *rod of God's anger*, so to Jeremiah is Babylon. God is using Babylon to punish His wicked and rebellious people. Like Assyria she, too, in her turn will fall; but, for the time, she is fulfilling God's purpose. He has given His once loved children into the hands of their enemies. This conviction never leaves Jeremiah. He has faith in God as the God of history; and when he is mocked and scorned because of the delay in the disaster which he prophesies, he yet stands firm in his awful declarations.

One of the most moving passages in Jeremiah's book is contained in a letter which he writes to the captives finally led away to Babylon by Nebuchadnezzar. This letter, remarkable for its common sense as well as for its hope, was apparently carried to them by the son of a man named

Shaphan, one of the few friends who had remained loyal
to Jeremiah. In it Jeremiah begs the captives to make the
best of their lot, even though it may continue through their
lifetime as a punishment meet for their sins. Nevertheless,
he tells them, they are to build new homes in Babylon, plant
gardens, marry and bring up children, contribute always
to the welfare of their alien land; for God who loved them
in the past longs to be merciful toward them, once they
repent of their transgressions and turn again to Him.

In the midst of his anger and despair Jeremiah proclaims
in countless passages throughout his book a message of
hope for the future of both Judah and Israel. Some especially beautiful verses in chapters 30 and 31 describe a New
Covenant which God will make with His people, a Covenant in which all shall know Him once again "from the
least of them unto the greatest." These redemptive poems
seem forerunners of the poetry of Isaiah of Babylon, who
fifty years later was to lend similar hope and courage to the
exiles there. Perhaps this Isaiah knew them and was but
echoing in his even greater literary genius the undying faith
of Jeremiah.

Many students and readers of Jeremiah have seen in him
not so much a teacher of religious truths, not so much a
prophet, as a great human personality. To them he sym-
bolizes the awakened mind of man, often doubting, seldom
free from fear, yet dead and useless without devotion, even
dedication to a Power beyond itself which alone gives
meaning to human life. His very cursing of that life, the
torment and anguish of his soul, his bitter loneliness, speak
to thoughtful men and women of every age. His unanswered
and unanswerable questions become their own; and he himself not only the most compassionate and companionable

of the prophets, but in a very real sense the symbol and the image of every man in his restless, never-ending search after "the things of God."

6

Isaiah of Babylon

THE MAN whom we call the Second Isaiah, or Isaiah of Babylon, because we have no knowledge of his real name, was in many ways a poet rather than a prophet. His actual prophecies are, indeed, only two: first, that the exiles in Babylonia shall return to Jerusalem and Judea; and second, that God, the One and Only Lord of all nations, shall at last become known as such by all men. Perhaps even these subjects are subjects of poetry rather than of prophecy in its true sense; and he is constantly transfiguring them into incomparable literary forms. Yet Isaiah of Babylon is rightly included among the great prophets because of the depth and the freshness of his ideas and convictions and because of the transformation which through them he gave to the thought and to the life of all Israel.

His work, as we have already learned, forms a part of the book of the real Isaiah. It is contained in chapters 40 to 55; and it probably includes also chapters 34 and 35 since these chapters, as we have also seen, reflect quite clearly his manner and his thought. What do we know about him?

We actually know very little; yet that little serves to characterize him; and we can safely infer a good deal more from his manner of writing, from his distinctive themes and his wealth of imagery, and from the situation in which he obviously lived and worked. His use of language, his way of teaching, surely suggests that he was a *young* man, endowed with strength, enthusiasm, and hope. We can quite as surely place him in Babylon among the Judean exiles there; and since he refers often to Cyrus, King of Media, who around 545 B.C. was threatening the power of Babylon and whom Isaiah of Babylon sees as a deliverer sent by God, we know that he was a contemporary of Cyrus.

His purpose throughout his book, which should be regarded as his own and in no sense belonging to Isaiah of Jerusalem, is to lend reassurance and cheer to those exiles who still hold, or have returned to their ancient faith and who are longing to return home. Babylon had not been unkind to them. They had been allowed to live in their own communities, to practice their own religion, to pursue their own ways and means of life; yet the devout among them, or among their children, were deeply conscious of their former guilt and sin as the people of God and were just as deeply homesick for their native land.

This Isaiah of Babylon may well have lived in one of the communities set apart for the original exiles; and his parents, or perhaps his grandparents, may well have been among those captives led away from Jerusalem and Judea in 587 B.C. His many references to the history of a united Israel as a people, to patriarchal figures, Noah, Abraham, Jacob, to the bondage in Egypt, and to other Old Testament events, prove that he was steeped in that history. He knew

Babylon, too, its heathen worship, its sorcerers, its astrologers, its magical rites and customs.

Like Jeremiah, he was a keen observer of nature and clearly a lover of the country. His poems are filled with trees, the cedar, cypress, oak, ash, and myrtle, the "willows by the water courses." He, too, knew the habits of birds, the cormorant, the bittern, the ravens, and the owls. Nothing escapes him, not even the reeds and rushes of the pools, the treasures of the darkness, the rain and the snow, the hidden riches of "secret places." In his imagination, his quick, intimate personification, the mountains and hills "break forth into singing" and all the trees of the field "clap their hands."

He has watched, too, the life of men in the streets of towns and cities, the many kinds of work which they do. He knows how the smith uses his tongs and his hammers; how the baker places his loaves in the oven; how the carpenter draws careful lines upon his wood; how the goldsmith casts his chains of gold and silver; and how the water-carrier calls out to the thirsty in the market-place. There is in his poetry an innate respect for all these simple men who, in the later words of the Apocryphal book of Ecclesiasticus, uphold "the fabric of the world" and whose prayer is in the work of their hands.

Isaiah of Babylon seems always to stand between the old and seemingly ruined world of Israel and one which is new; and the task to which he dedicates his life is to see the old transcended *by* the new, its faith reborn by a new understanding of the God of its fathers. He is the first not only of the prophets, but of all the writers of the Old Testament to understand and to proclaim that God is not alone the God of history and the God of Israel, but the Lord of all men. Thus he widens both the early vision of Amos, who taught that God had brought other peoples out of bondage, and the theme of Isaiah of Jerusalem, who saw Him as the *Holy One of Israel*, by declaring that He is the Lord of the whole earth. Before Him "all inhabitants are as grasshoppers"; and in His eyes the islands are "a very little thing."

To this all-enfolding prophetic idea he adds his particular conception of God as the *Redeemer* of Israel. This term, which he uses in verse after verse of his poetry, unites memory with expectation. The memories of those who hear him reach back into the past, to the Exodus from Egypt, to the Covenant at Sinai, to the ancient meaning of the very word *redemption*, the ransom willingly paid for a kinsman by the closest member of his family. Thus God becomes once more the head of His family, ready with His ransom, the father of His repentant children, the shepherd of His flock.

It is significant that Isaiah of Babylon begins his book with the word *comfort*. Nor does this comfort mean merely consolation. Inherent in his use of it is the sense of encouragement, of hope, and of expectation. In an impassioned series of images he describes the protection with which God as redeemer will lead His people back homeward across the desert. He will make the mountains easier to ascend, the dry valleys less perilous, the "crooked paths straight," the "rough places plain." Water will spring forth from the parched ground; the wilderness and the solitary places will rejoice and blossom. God will lead His people as a shepherd leads his flock. He will carry the children in

His arms and take especial care of those women who are soon to become mothers.

Like the author of Job, this poet of Babylon marvels over the mighty works of God as the Creator of the Universe. He seems to have paved the way for those young men in the fiery furnace who magnify all God's wondrous works as they walk unharmed upon the glowing coals. For his entire book is another *Benedicite*, as we shall see in a later chapter given to its study.

Lastly, in chapter 53 he gives expression to a new and startling thought in his interpretation of the meaning of human suffering. All the sufferings borne by the exiles he sees as a means of blessing, not only to themselves but to others. Even punishment, borne with dignity and patience, results, he teaches, in new vitality and power. It may, in fact, become a vicarious sacrifice for the sins and sufferings of those who have been contemptuous and scornful of the punished, rejected, and despised Israelites.

This doctrine of vicarious suffering was so new to its time as to be cataclysmic. Did it have its inspired source only in the sad heart of Isaiah of Babylon as he went about among his anxious, repentant people and strove after new ways to lend them hope? Was it but a means of added comfort and courage? Was it, perhaps, a natural furtherance of his insistence that God had forgiven and redeemed them, had planned for them a new and glorious future in recompense for their pain and sorrow? Or was it, instead, as many have believed through the ages, a vision born of a rich, unfettered imagination, the vision of the possible healing and vitalizing influence of human anguish, of a people or of an individual, upon the lives and the thoughts of others?

Whatever the answers to these questions, or whatever the interpretation of chapter 53 of his book, this revelation of the vicarious nature of suffering, together with his teaching of complete monotheism, marks Isaiah of Babylon as the poet and the prophet of a New Age for the people of Israel.

PART THREE

Hebrew Prophecy as Literature

1

Literary Manners
of the Prophets

AMONG THE many values awaiting readers and students of the great Hebrew prophets is the realization of the impressive individualism of each, an individualism which, I hope, has been already made evident in the foregoing portraits of them. In background, environment, personality, interests, speech, every one of them is singularly himself. Even Amos and Micah, both countrymen, both accustomed to utmost simplicity of life, both inured to hard, manual work, reveal unmistakably original characteristics in their respective attitudes toward their callings and in their use of language, just as do Isaiah of Jerusalem and Jeremiah, although they, too, resemble each other in their similar backgrounds and in their common native gifts.

Nevertheless, with all their intense individualism as men and as teachers and leaders, all our great prophets share certain ways of expression, certain linguistic devices, certain literary manners. Perhaps it is more accurate to say that these expressions, these devices, these manners are characteristic of Hebrew prophecy as a type of ancient literature—in other words, that the best of the prophets of Israel, like the best of her psalmists, make use of the same or similar means of expression in order to ensure the same effects. Or, to put it in yet another way, that prophecy is made effective largely by the conscious employment of several distinctive methods of composition, whether that composition was, in the beginning, oral or written.

What, then, are the chief and the most interesting of these literary methods and manners? By what means did the prophets impress their hearers centuries ago, and in what specific ways do they still impress their readers?

The most characteristic prophetic utterance was, and *is* the *oracle*, which may be defined as (1) a fervent appeal for the realization of a wrong and dangerous condition or situation and (2) a plea for its change, its cure, by the transformation of the minds and souls of men. This *oracle* in the addresses of all the prophets of Israel and Judah followed a definite pattern. It is impossible today to be entirely sure how far the prophets themselves were responsible for the form in which we now read their oracles; yet, although later editors may have reconstructed or brought together certain passages, there is no valid reason to assume that the prophetic speaker, or writer, did not consciously use this form, this literary pattern, or that he did not fully realize its power and effectiveness.

This pattern of the oracle is made up of three distinctive features. The oracle usually begins with a *declaration* of the condition deplored by the prophet; continues with a *reproach* or an *exhortation* to the people responsible for this condition; and concludes with a *threat* or a *promise* of God's

retribution in the imminent, or the distant future. Not in-
frequently one of these features precedes or is combined
with another; yet each is always clearly distinguishable. The
tone or the atmosphere in which the oracle is uttered depends, of course, upon the nature and character of the
prophet himself, upon his anger, his grief, his despair, or his
hope, in other words upon what manner of man he was.

A recognition of these distinctive features, an ability to
discern them in the units of composition to which they supply the pattern, will add immeasurably to the intelligent
reading of the prophetic books. A few illustrations here
may be helpful. More will be given with notes and comments in the Selections quoted in Part IV of this book.

Amos in his chapter 5 utters one of his many oracles in
the austerity and the anger always characteristic of him.
One readily sees in this oracle the three features already
described:

> I know your manifold transgressions and your mighty sins:
> They afflict the just, they take a bribe,
> They turn aside the poor in the gate from their right.
> Therefore, the prudent shall keep silence in that time;
> For it is an evil time.
>
> Seek good and not evil that ye may live;
> And so that the Lord, the God of hosts, shall be with you.
> Hate the evil, and love the good,
> And establish judgment in the gate.
>
> Therefore, the Lord, the God of hosts, the Lord saith this:
> Wailing shall be in all streets;
> And they shall say in all the highways, Alas! alas! . . . .
> And in all vineyards shall be wailing;
> For I will pass through thee, saith the Lord.

Woe unto you that desire the day of the Lord!
To what end is it for you?
The day of the Lord is darkness, and not light.

Even Hosea's usual tone of mercy and hope leaves him in his brief oracle in chapter 4 of his book, in which his *exhortation* and *reproach* are combined with his *declaration* of sin and wickedness:

Hear the word of the Lord, ye children of Israel!
For the Lord hath a controversy with the inhabitants of
   the land
Because there is no truth, nor mercy,
Nor knowledge of God in the land.
By swearing and lying and killing,
And stealing and committing adultery,
They break out, and blood toucheth blood.

Therefore shall the land mourn,
And everyone that dwelleth therein shall languish
With the beasts of the field and with the fowls of heaven;
Yea, the fishes of the sea also shall be taken away.

Micah in his turn vents his irony, rage, and hatred upon those in high position at Jerusalem. He cries out in chapter 3 of his book:

Hear this, I pray you, ye heads of the house of Jacob,
And princes of the house of Israel,
That abhor judgment and pervert all equity.
They build up Zion with blood
And Jerusalem with iniquity.
The heads thereof judge for reward,
And the priests thereof teach for hire,
And the prophets thereof divine for money.
Yet they will lean upon the Lord, and say:

Is not the Lord among us?
No evil can come upon us.

Therefore, shall Zion for your sake be plowed as a field,
And Jerusalem shall become heaps,
And the mountain of the house as the high places of the
*   forest.*

Isaiah of Jerusalem in one of his finest oracles echoes
promises together with his threats, promises which lend a
healing note to God's awful questions and accusations.
Here the pattern of the prophetic oracle is seen at its best
with its three clearly recognizable features, its *declaration,*
its *exhortation,* its *promise:*

To what purposes is the multitude of your sacrifices unto
*   me? saith the Lord.*
I am full of the burnt offerings of rams, and the fat of fed
*   beasts!*
I delight not in the blood of bullocks, or of lambs, or of
*   he-goats!*
When ye come to appear before me,
Who hath required this at your hand?
Incense is an abomination unto me.
Your new moons and your appointed feasts my soul hateth.
They are a trouble unto me; I am weary to bear them.
Your hands are full of blood.

Wash ye, and make you clean.
Put away the evil of your doings from before my eyes.
Learn to do well. Seek judgment, relieve the oppressed,
Judge the fatherless, plead for the widow.

Come now, and let us reason together, saith the Lord.
Though your sins be as scarlet, they shall be white as snow;
Though they be red like crimson, they shall be as wool.

*If ye be willing and obedient, ye shall eat the good of the
    land;*
*But if ye refuse and rebel, ye shall be devoured with the
    sword;*
For the mouth of the Lord hath spoken it.

Although the oracle is the most outstanding literary expression of the prophetic books, there are many other
dramatic uses of language, constructions which not only
contribute vividness and variety to the style, but which
also serve to characterize the individual writers. One of
these constructions, used by all the classical prophets, yet
by each after his own manner, is the rhetorical question.
Such a form of language is actually not so much a question
as it is an interrogative comment, the weight or the burden
of which is conveyed in the form of a question in order to
enlist sharply the attention of the hearer or the reader, perhaps even to startle him.

Rhetorical questions are, of course, in no sense peculiar
only to the prophets. They occur again and again throughout the Old Testament in both its prose and poetry. And
yet the prophets use them with such extreme sensitiveness
and power that it would be a thousand pities not to become
acutely aware of them in their writings. And there is no
one of their literary manners which portray them quite so
clearly and distinctly as individuals.

Such questions serve Amos admirably in his outbursts of
fury and scorn: *The lion hath roared, who will not fear?
Shall not the land tremble for this, and everyone mourn
that dwelleth therein? Are ye not as children of the Ethiopians unto me?* And Micah, like Amos, sounds his contempt
and hatred when he cries: *What are the high places of
Judah? Are they not Jerusalem?*

The rhetorical questions of Hosea and Jeremiah reveal them also as they were, sad, even heartbroken men who suffer with their people and within whose words pity and sorrow linger. *How shall I give thee up, Ephraim?* asks Hosea. *How shall I deliver thee, Israel?* And two of Jeremiah's countless questions convey the depths of his misery in their plaintive, haunting accents: *Is there no balm in Gilead? Is there no physician there?*

In the mind and the pen of Isaiah of Jerusalem these rhetorical questions suggest his swift changes of mood. In one, he is accusing and angry: *What mean ye that ye beat my people to pieces, and grind the faces of the poor?* In another, he is desperate and hopeless: *O house of David, Is it a small thing for you to weary men, but will ye weary my God also?* In others, his fear wars with his pleading: *And what will ye do in the desolation which shall come from afar? To whom will ye flee for help? And where will ye leave your glory?* And, finally, he is as puzzled and sorrowful as were Hosea and Jeremiah, when he makes God ask in a broken, human voice: *What could have been done more to my vineyard that I have not done in it? Wherefore, when I looked that it should bring forth grapes, brought it forth wild grapes?*

The prophets are masters also of mockery, of taunts, and of considered insults. The authors of the books of Job and of Ecclesiastes mock also; but they are not so skilled in the language of biting scorn as are the prophets. Sometimes this mockery is used in a scathing, satirical invitation. Amos does this to perfection:

> *Come to Bethel and transgress!*
> *At Gilgal multiply transgressions!*

> *Bring your sacrifices every morning,*
> *And your tithes after three years!*

And although Jeremiah is perhaps less direct in his bitterness than Amos, his invitation, too, is a mocking one:

> *Thus saith the Lord of hosts:*
> *Call for the mourning women that they may come,*
> *And send for cunning women that they may come.*
> *Let them make haste and take up a wailing for us*
> *That our eyes may run down with tears,*
> *And our eyelids gush out with waters.*

At other times the prophets make use of epithets to express their sarcastic mockery. Many of these epithets are terrible in their taunting quality and in their humiliating references to past history or to present familiar things, well known to the people of Israel and Judah. Thus Isaiah employs traditional wicked cities to which to liken the inhabitants of Jerusalem:

> *Hear the word of the Lord, ye rulers of Sodom!*
> *Give ear unto the law of our God, ye people of Gomorrah!*

Amos not only uses stupid cows to characterize the selfish, dissipated women of Israel, but heightens his scornful comparison by choosing the fattest cows known to them, those which feed in the rich pastures of Bashan:

> *Hear this word, ye kine of Bashan,*
> *That are in the mountains of Samaria,*
> *Which oppress the poor, which crush the needy,*
> *Which say to their masters, Bring, and let us drink!*

Nor do the prophets in their genius at mockery refrain even from grim and ironic jokes at the expense of their hearers. Knowing full well those personal indulgences and extravagances which the people of both the northern and the southern kingdom have come to value, they take pains in their threats to make sport of these falsely cherished habits and ways of life. Amos declares God's fury against their vanities when he cries:

> *I will turn your feasts into mourning*
> *And all your songs into lamentations.*
> *I will bring sackcloth upon all loins,*
> *And baldness upon every head.*

And Isaiah of Jerusalem echoes him when he warns the silly women of Jerusalem of the prices they will pay for their unbridled devotion to perfumes, to fine fabrics, and to visits to the hairdresser:

> *Instead of sweet smell, there shall be stink,*
> *And instead of a girdle, a rent;*
> *Instead of well-set hair, baldness,*
> *And instead of a stomacher, a girding of sackcloth.*

Puns, or clever plays on words, were apparently enjoyed by the prophets. We have already noted this play on words in the names which Hosea and Isaiah of Jerusalem gave to their children, names symbolic of future happenings. Other examples of such word-play occur under other circumstances.

Readers of English can hardly appreciate these as did those who listened to them in their native Hebrew; yet they must not be overlooked, since to the prophets they were evidently full of meaning and designed carefully in order to impress their hearers. They occur mostly in the visions which the prophets describe; and they must have struck home pertinently to those who listened.

In his 8th chapter Amos describes a basket of summer fruit, which God brings before his eyes. The subtle portent of this vision is lost unless we realize that the word for such *fruit* in transliterated Hebrew is *kais* and that the same word, at least in its pronunciation, *kes*, means *destruction*. Therefore, this vision of Amos held a two-fold significance, surely both obvious and disturbing to his hearers. Jeremiah employs the same play upon words when he relates his vision of a blossoming almond tree. This almond tree in Hebrew is *shaquedh;* and it is closely related in form to the Hebrew word for one who awakens or who watches, the word *shoquedh*. As a further example, Isaiah of Jerusalem in his lovely song of God's vineyard employs this apt sense of diction by using the word for justice, *mishpat*, in close connection with its exact opposite, the word for oppression, or *mispah*. Although such pairs of words may mean little to us today, we may be sure that their significance was both clear and caustic to those who heard them in the speech of the prophets.

2

Perhaps this study of the literary manners and methods of the prophets has, thus far at least, tended to emphasize the rather ruthless brilliance of their minds, their darker, more austere aspects as teachers and leaders. Such an understanding of them would be both incomplete and quite unfair. All of them possessed profound and lovely poetic qualities, rich imaginations, the quick perception of all "ancient, beautiful things" in the world about them, in the manifold gifts of Nature and in the old ways of life which the country people had followed for many generations. The four earlier prophets, Amos, Hosea, Isaiah of Jerusalem, and Micah, and the later Jeremiah were, it is true, far lesser poets than was Isaiah of Babylon; and yet all were extremely sensitive in aesthetic appreciation and in its expression. All wrote noble poetry, each in his own distinctive fashion.

Let us now, then, consider those literary manners which reveal them primarily as poets rather than as preachers. The first of these may well be their *use of images*, their reference to those objects or events in their experience which clearly held most meaning and appeal both to them and to their hearers.

The images used by Amos are, for the most part, images of the barren desert country which was his home, the animals which he knew—those he cared for, his sheep, those he feared, lions, bears, serpents; the rocks and stones which made his ways difficult; the years of famine which he endured; the plagues of insects. These images are without exception stark, directly presented, often menacing. Fire is obviously his favourite image, for he uses it again and again and always with strength. His trees, too, are tall and strong; and he takes pains to emphasize the iron of farming implements. Such images in themselves contribute to the inflexible strength and power of his poetry.

Hosea's images are of an entirely different nature. Instead of being harsh and inflexible, they are gentle and strangely muted. They seem dim and even fragile in comparison with those of Amos. Hosea's trees cast pleasant shadows. He clearly loved other frail and shadowy things: smoke from chimneys, morning clouds, foam upon water, early dew upon the grass. His most frequently used images are comforting and pleasing: corn, wine, and oil; and he even speaks of their scent and fragrance. He *can*, upon occasion, be austere and stern; his lions *can* devour; his winds *can* become whirlwinds. Yet most of the imagery throughout his book is marked by a singular gentleness. To him the doves seem "silly"; and the birds which fly often above his pages are "the fowls of heaven."

Isaiah of Jerusalem, as we shall see more clearly in the following chapter, was profuse and prodigal in his poetry. There is no sure labelling of him or of his images either as austere or as gentle. As his moods change, as mercy banishes revenge, so do his images change. Fire, desolate valleys, ragged rocks, dark caves, ruined cities give place to fruitful hills, friendly, companionable beasts, butter and honey, softly-flowing waters. Unlike Micah, whose violent imagination saw fire and blood, dragons and owls, floods and mighty torrents, heard wailings and howlings, this Isaiah from time to time knew the delights of "pleasant pictures"; ships returning from foreign shores; dreams of an age of peace for all nations. Such realities were without doubt rare in his troubled life; dark images are far more plentiful in his poetry than are those suffused by light; yet the bright ones *do* occur, and they contribute greatly to the remarkable variety of his diction and his style.

The fifty-two chapters of the book of Jeremiah abound in imagery; and since their authorship is far less open to question than is that of the many chapters of the book of Isaiah, their contents can be studied with much greater confidence —that is, we can be far more sure of Jeremiah's own interests and enthusiasms. As we have already learned from his portrait, Jeremiah was the most candid, the least reserved of all the prophets; and, as we might well expect, his wealth of imagery contributes generously to this impression of him. Now, images darken his pages: images of death, its shadow and its terrors; images of warfare, battlements, fortresses, fire, swords, lances, famine, chariots and horses. Now, they brighten his many verses: images of waters, of fountains, of the light of the moon and the stars, even the light of a homely household candle. There are many images of music, the sound of trumpets and of pipes, the singing of birds. More images have to do with voices of many sorts.

Just as Amos is consumed by the thought of fire, and as Hosea clearly loves the shadowy and the fragile, so Jeremiah is obviously haunted by many and various voices. Perhaps they held unusual meaning for him since in the beginning of his ministry, as we recall, he distrusted the power of his own voice to speak in behalf of God. Whether or not such an idea is more than a tantalizing fancy, Jeremiah's many voices which echo throughout his book are a certainty. These voices appear again and again: voices of merriment and thanksgiving; the menacing and terrifying voice of Babylon; voices of mirth and gladness; the voice of a woman in travail, which is the voice of the daughter of Zion; voices of weeping and lamentation, that voice of Rachel in Ramah; the voice of living waters.

More often than all other voices, so frequent, indeed, as to be inescapable, are wedding voices, "the voice of the bride" and "the voice of the bridegroom." These wedding voices are repeated, reiterated, as though Jeremiah's desire that all should hear them can never be fully satisfied. Are they perhaps reminiscent of his own sacrifice of marriage for the sake of his ministry?

Images, of course, as all readers are aware, form the basis for figures of speech, for *similes, metaphors, personification*. A simile or a metaphor is, in fact, a double image, by which the poet intensifies or clarifies his original object or image by comparing or likening it to another, and by this comparison adds to its meaning, endows it with new and fresh reality. Such comparisons occur throughout the prophetic books and add immeasurably to their vividness and drama. Like the single image, only with greater strength, they suggest the personality of those who use them; reveal the distinctive imagination of each prophet as a poet; and in this way contribute charm and character to his work.

Amos increases God's weariness with the people of Israel by saying that under the burden of that weariness He is like a cart which is pressed too full of sheaves. In a similar country metaphor he declares that God will sift His rebellious people as a farmer sifts corn through a sieve. And in an even stronger comparison this prophet of disaster sees Israel as a blazing piece of wood in the fire of God's anger. To Hosea, not once but twice, the former faith of Israel and Judah has become like a fading cloud at dawn and like the fleetingness of early dew. When God shall roar in His just anger like a lion, His children shall tremble like frightened birds which fall from the skies; and all their past glory shall flee away, again like the fowls of the heavens. To Isaiah of Jerusalem, in a hopeless moment, the daughter of Zion is like a desolate cottage in a vineyard; and, in a hopeful one, the knowledge of God shall at last cover the earth as the waters cover the sea. Jeremiah's figures are as numerous as are his single images. He likens the indifferent people of Judah and Jerusalem to broken cisterns which hold no water, whereas God is the fountain of living waters. Again, they are like stubble which shall be scattered by the whirlwinds of God's anger; or they are like wandering sheep which know no shepherd; or they are like thirsty children who can find no water; or they are like wild asses which have no grass to crop. In perhaps the most moving of Jeremiah's countless similes God is like a stranger in His own land, like a wayfaring man who looks in vain for a lodging for the night.

The figure of speech known as *personification* is far less prevalent in the poetry of the five earlier prophets than it is in that of Isaiah of Babylon where it becomes one of his most outstanding and revealing literary expressions. By means of this figure, a poet endows the creations of God in Nature with human and personal behaviour. Sometimes he calls upon these creations, earth and sky, moon and stars, mountains and hills, to lend their voices in praise or lamentation, in mourning or in astonishment, in fear or in wonder; at other times he describes them as doing so. The psalmists, as we all know, were lavish users of personification. Certain of the prophets, on the contrary, are conspicuously lacking in it. The brief books of Amos, Hosea, and Micah, probably because of their length, contain almost none of it; and Isaiah of Jerusalem, in the chapters generally accorded to him, rarely employs it. Jeremiah, on the other hand, in the lavish and unrestrained language always characteristic of him, often uses this ecstatic figure of speech. He describes the earth as *mourning* and the heavens as *astonished*. Both earth and sky *cry out* for the destruction of Babylon; and the land of Judah *sorrows* over the wickedness of her people.

3

These literary manners which I have tried to define and analyze are the most frequent and outstanding of the many methods used by the prophets to impress the words of God upon their hearers. The distinctive manner of utterance, the tones and the rhythm of voice peculiar to each, have also been suggested in the portraits drawn of them as individuals. The two chapters which follow and which conclude this book will deal more fully with the literary work of those two prophets whose writings have for many centuries justly received the wonder and the admiration of countless readers: Isaiah of Jerusalem and the later Isaiah, known as Isaiah of Babylon.

2

Isaiah of Jerusalem as a Stylist

THE LONG history of literature, through all ages and in many countries, is marked now and again by artists who are able to write not only in one literary form, but in many, who constantly surprise their readers by their extraordinary versatility, both in the nature of their material and in the manner of their expression. Their talents are unbounded. They are not merely poets, or story-tellers, or essayists, or dramatists. They seem, singularly enough, to do all things well.

Such a writer was the Roman poet, Ausonius, who lived in the fourth century A.D., whose home was in Gaul, in Bordeaux, and who was very likely Celtic by descent. He was not in any sense a great artist; probably few persons today read him at all, to their own loss, for his work possesses real charm even for the most modern of readers. His stature was far from that of Horace, or of Virgil, or of Catullus, who himself was skillful in his use of many subjects and of many metrical forms. Yet Ausonius is justly remembered because he could put his hand and his mind to a vast variety of literary expressions from epitaphs and riddles to portraiture, letters, epigrams, and poetry on Nature. He was also clearly given to sudden changes of mood, from the austere and the solemn to the buoyant and the arch.

Such another artist was, of course, Shakespeare, who could with equal skill write blank verse; or sonnets; or the dialogue of shoemakers, witches, gravediggers; or ballads; or lyrical songs. Thomas Hardy, renowned rightly as a novelist, was a poet as well, with an unlimited variety of metres, and also a dramatist. Robert Louis Stevenson owes his perhaps questionable literary fame not so much to his enduring power over words as to his versatile employment of them, in memorable and exciting stories, in essays, and in poems beloved by children. A score of other writers will, of course, spring to the minds of all lovers of books. These are but a few obvious examples of those possessed by marked skill and dexterity in the use of language.

Isaiah of Jerusalem belongs among these masters of many forms; and he, like Catullus and Shakespeare, was an artist rather than merely a craftsman. More than any other of the prophets he was gifted with an amazing command of style. Although as a master of Hebrew poetry he does not rank with his namesake, Isaiah of Babylon, he, nevertheless, excelled the later Isaiah in his prodigal number of literary forms and in his astonishing range of material. He could and did write superb descriptive and narrative prose; he was talented also in the composition of songs; of satires; of lyrics; and of oracles of various sorts. All these quite different, even disparate, literary types he crams into the few chapters of his book which are acknowledged to be his own, and constantly surprises his readers by some new and fresh

expression of his facile, eclectic genius. Nothing in the
shape of words daunted him. And for this reason he is
justly remembered as among the most rich and varied styl-
ists in any language.

To wonder about the source of this remarkable power is
irresistible, even though its discovery is impossible because
of the little reliable information which we have concerning
him. Did his power spring from his wide social contacts,
from his observation, at once quick and profound, of men
and women and their always fascinating ways? How much
did his life in Jerusalem contribute to it? His education, his
family, his social position, his acquaintance with the nearby
countryside? One must suppose that he was devoted to
music, surely sacred, perhaps secular as well. His imagination seems to have possessed that rare synthetic quality
which enabled him to bring together the old and the new,
to fuse them until they became a single vast treasure-house
of riches: on the one hand, the long, God-shadowed history
of his people; on the other, things as simple and familiar as
the pool of Shiloah, or as the ass in "his master's crib," or
as those children who were rude to their elders. Perhaps
we can safely assume that his life, with all its sorrows and
tragedies, was in Matthew Arnold's words "so various, so
beautiful, so new" that it demanded forms various and
beautiful and new in which to be expressed.

His prose is memorable not only because of its directness,
its seeming simplicity, but because of the singular impression of height, of loftiness which it conveys. This sense
of height is gained by the subordination of relatively unimportant constructions in order that the most telling parts
of speech, the nouns and the verbs, may hold the most
important position in his sentences. It is gained also by his

use of words, vivid and dramatic in themselves. Nowhere is this effect better shown than in his story of his vision in the Temple. A study of this description, included in the Selections quoted in Part IV of this book, will reveal this sense of height so characteristic of him. And we should surely note in passing that the English of the Authorized Version has almost miraculously managed to retain the loftiness, the exaltation of the original Hebrew.

Like his prose, the poetry of Isaiah of Jerusalem also constantly conveys this sense of height. One of his single verses, which appears in chapter 9 and which seems peculiarly isolated from its context, affords another admirable example of this quality in the careful choice and the equally careful placing of important words in order to ensure this effect:

> *The people that walked in darkness*
> *Have seen a great light.*
> *They that dwelt in the land of the shadow of death,*
> *Upon them hath the light shined.*

Isaiah of Jerusalem was peculiarly sensitive to poetic rhythm, even to melody (and unmistakable melody was rare among Hebrew writers). In Chapter 5 of his book he writes a song, quite consciously, for he calls it *A Song of God's Vineyard*. It is, moreover, accented after the manner of a musical composition. The final verse given here is sufficient to illustrate his control over language in quite another form, his sense of rhythm and of accent:

> *For the vineyard of the Lord of hosts is the house of Israel,*
> *And the men of Judah his pleasant plant.*
> *And he looked for jud'gment, but, behold! oppression;*
> *For ri'ghteousness, but, beh'old! a cry.*

He was a master, too, of bitter irony and satire, in which his piercing words burst forth, now in prose, now in staccato-like poetry, words supported by only a few carefully chosen adjectives, yet complete and terrible in themselves. Nowhere is this power over satire seen so well as in his diatribe against the women of Jerusalem with the ornaments of their vanity and with their arrogant pride. Written in both prose and poetry, it remains, among the many instances of irony in Old Testament literature, perhaps the most effective in its terse catalogue of objects doomed to destruction along with their stupid wearers. Its opening paragraph in prose is memorable in its succinctness:

In that day the Lord will take away the bravery of their tinkling ornaments about their feet, and their cauls, and their round tires like the moon. The chains and the bracelets and the mufflers; the bonnets and the ornaments of the legs, and the headbands, and the tablets, and the ear-rings; the rings and nose jewels; the changeable suits of apparel, and the mantles, and the wimples, and the crisping pins; the glasses, and the fine linen, and the hoods, and the veils.

The objects given here are impressive largely because of their stark and simple concreteness, their very lack of accompanying descriptive words. All Hebrew writers, and especially those of its earlier literature, used few adjectives; their language was singularly wanting in them, doubtless *because* they felt little need of them. They preferred to rely upon the strength of the nouns and verbs. In this passage the glasses (hand-mirrors), the cauls (head-bands), the round tires (probably necklaces), the mufflers (scarfs) obviously seemed vivid enough to Isaiah in his fierce catalogue of them. He was quite right and wise in letting them stand largely alone, unqualified by adjectives.

Swift changes in mood and atmosphere are characteristic of this Isaiah's style. Immediately following his attack upon the women of Jerusalem comes his moving description of a future when God shall once more return to Mount Zion, when the sins of its people shall have been purged as by cleansing fire. Here his aesthetic sense determines his choice of words, governs alike his images and metaphors and the length of his lines:

> *In that day shall the branch of the Lord be beautiful and*
> *glorious,*
> *And the fruit of the earth shall be excellent and*
> *comely. . . .*
> *And it shall come to pass that he that is left in Zion*
> *And he that remaineth in Jerusalem*
> *Shall be called holy. . . .*
>
> *And the Lord will create upon every dwelling place of*
> *Mount Zion*
> *A cloud and smoke by day,*
> *And the shining of a flaming fire by night . . .*
> *And there shall be a tabernacle for a shadow in the day-*
> *time from the heat,*
> *And for a place of refuge,*
> *And for a covert from storm and from rain.*

A sense of drama always pervades the work of Isaiah of Jerusalem, both in his prose and in his poetry. His poem on the coming of the Assyrians supplies a good example of this dramatic sense, which is clearly evident in his apt choice of words, his distinctive imagery, and his fine use of comparisons, as well as in the accelerated pace of his language:

And he will lift up an ensign to the nations from far
And will hiss unto them from the end of the earth;
And, behold! they shall come with speed swiftly.
None shall be weary nor stumble among them,
None shall slumber nor sleep. . . .
Their arrows are sharp, and all their bows bent,
Their horses' hoofs shall be counted like flint,
And their wheels like a whirlwind.
Their roaring shall be like a lion,
They shall roar like young lions.
Yea, they shall roar and lay hold of their prey,
And shall carry it away safe,
And none shall deliver it.

And if one look unto the land, behold! darkness and sorrow.
And the light is darkened in the heavens thereof.

When one considers the fact, already noted, that in the long book named for him, only a few chapters can be established as without question his own, this perceptive understanding of language, this versatile use of it in many differing forms, becomes not only of vast interest, but of great value in any study of him as a literary artist. Of all the prophets he knew best how to adapt his style to his subject; and because of this gift he merits especial attention and study.

In one of his critical essays Thomas De Quincey defines words as the *incarnation of thoughts*. This definition Isaiah of Jerusalem understood and illustrated both in his prose and his poetry. Not to be aware of his unique power in the selection and use of those words deprives his readers of understanding and pleasure and fails to give the prophet himself the literary distinction which he rightly deserves.

3

Isaiah of Babylon as a Poet

READERS OF this book will do well (and also give themselves incomparable pleasure) if they will read at one *uninterrupted* time chapters 40 to 55, inclusive, of the book of Isaiah. These chapters, together most probably with chapters 34 and 35, comprise the work of that prophet and poet who is called Isaiah of Babylon and who is held by many to be the finest literary artist of the Old Testament. In this concluding chapter of my book I shall try to make that suggested reading of him more intelligent and pleasurable by stressing certain qualities of his poetry. These qualities are in no sense exhaustive or even thoroughly analyzed; his poetry is far too rich and varied for us to study *all* its many features and aspects; but I believe that those which I am presenting here are the most characteristic of their author and also distinctive and peculiar to his work.

Isaiah of Babylon is rightly numbered among our great prophets, for he believed devoutly in a new age for the people of Israel once they had atoned for their sins; and, as we have seen in his portrait, he contributed fresh and most valuable ideas on the nature of God. Yet he is, first and foremost, a poet; and it is with the singular character of his poetry that we shall now concern ourselves. What were its most distinctive qualities? Why has it been revered and loved through many centuries, repeated, re-echoed, memorized, cherished?

Perhaps its most outstanding quality, one that brightens countless stanzas, is *its sense of the new,* of something which constantly surprises one, like a sudden glow of light banishing all darkness, all despair, all sorrow. This newness, these new and transforming acts which God will perform for His ransomed people, are expressed by Isaiah of Babylon in various ways. The most simple, concrete, and obvious of these is the use of the word itself or of its derivatives. He writes:

> *Remember not the former things,*
> *Neither consider the things of old,*
> *Behold! I will do a new thing.*
>
> *Behold! the former things are come to pass,*
> *And new things do I declare.*
>
> *Sing unto the Lord a new song*
> *And his praise from the end of the earth.*
>
> *They that wait upon the Lord shall renew their strength.*

Often, in place of the actual words, other terms, suggestive or symbolic of *newness,* are used by the poet to produce the same effect. *Tidings* is one of these; *light* is another; *redeem, see,* and *behold* are others:

> *How beautiful upon the mountains*
> *Are the feet of him that bringeth good tidings!*

O Zion that bringest good tidings,
Get thee up into the high mountains!
O Jerusalem that bringest good tidings,
Lift up thy voice with strength!

I will make darkness light before them,
And crooked things straight.

I am the Lord, and there is none else.
I form the light.

Fear not, for I have redeemed thee,
I have called thee by thy name.

Therefore the redeemed of the Lord shall return,
And come with singing unto Zion.

Lift up thine eyes round about, and behold!

Lift up your eyes to the heavens,
And look upon the earth beneath.

Hear, ye deaf, and look, ye blind,
That ye may see!

This *newness* is perhaps even more powerfully expressed by contrast, by lyrical figurative descriptions of the changes which will be brought about by the restored care and love of God. The eyes of the blind shall be opened; the ears of the deaf shall be unstopped; the dumb shall speak and sing; the lame man shall leap as a hart. Nor is this transformation limited to *persons* who have suffered guilt and shame. In the imagination of Isaiah of Babylon, it extends also to the creations of God in Nature. The barren desert will rejoice and blossom; the parched ground will bring forth water; shade trees will spring up in the wilderness. As the exiles start homeward on their long journey, the high mountains shall be made lower for their ascent; the dry, treacherous valleys shall be freed from ravenous beasts; the crooked, obscure paths shall be made straight, and the rough places plain.

Old fears have no longer any reality. Hope has transfigured them all. For God will make all things, whether men or mountains, *new*.

Throughout the poetry of Isaiah of Babylon there is, as a second quality, a prevailing *sense of exultation*. He calls upon everyone, and, indeed, upon every *thing* to *awake*, to *rejoice*, to *praise*. These imperatives, mostly musical in their imagery, lend, of course, a mounting character to his verse, which constantly rises through his fervent appeals and commands:

> *Sing, O ye heavens!*
> *Shout, ye lower parts of the earth!*
> *Break forth into singing, ye mountains!*
> *O forest, and every tree therein!*
>
> *Awake, awake, put on thy strength, O Zion!*
> *Put on thy beautiful garments, O Jerusalem, the holy city!*
>
> *Break forth into joy, ye waste places of Jerusalem!*
> *For the Lord hath comforted his people,*
> *He hath redeemed Jerusalem.*

Together with God's commands to His ransomed children are His promises, proclaimed in the same exultant and exalted strain:

> *For a small moment have I forsaken thee,*
> *But with great mercies will I gather thee.*

In a little wrath I hid my face from thee for a moment;
But with everlasting kindness will I have mercy on thee,
Saith the Lord, thy Redeemer.

These promises are frequently made more vivid by brilliant imagery of a new Jerusalem, imagery which reminds one, of course, of St. John's shining streets and jewelled gates and which was without doubt familiar to him when he wrote his vision six hundred years after the time of Isaiah of Babylon:

O thou afflicted, tossed with tempest, and not comforted,
Behold! I will lay thy stones with fair colours,
And lay thy foundations with sapphires.
And I will make thy windows of agates,
And thy gates of carbuncles,
And all thy borders of pleasant stones.

Personification often enforces these promises of God. Nature, too, shall rejoice in the return home of the exiles:

For ye shall go out with joy
And be led forth with peace.
The mountains and the hills shall break before you into
*   singing,*
And all the trees of the field shall clap their hands.

Yet with all his sense of the *new*, with all his exultant calls to praise, Isaiah of Babylon never forgets the old, those ancient days when the people of Israel knew the Covenant at Sinai, the early Mosaic faith. This third feature of his poetry, this remembrance of things past, haunts his verses, now with pathos, now with almost stern reminders of those former faithful years of Israel's history as a people:

Awake, awake, put on strength, O arm of the Lord!
Awake, as in the ancient days,
In the generations of old.

Rhetorical questions serve him well to bring back to his people this forgotten or forsaken knowledge of God. Again and again he asks such questions:

Have ye not known?
Have ye not heard?
Hath it not been told you from the beginning?
Have ye not understood from the foundations of the earth?

And, lastly this poet of Babylon stresses, as no one before him among all Old Testament writers had ever stressed, the *oneness* of God, the understanding that there is no other but Him revealed to Israel as the God of Righteousness and Justice, Holiness and Might, the Father of all men, yet their Ruler and their Judge. This theme binds all his poetry together, is the unifying motif of all his work. From chapter 40, which itself contains three clearly distinguishable poems, one on God's Reality, another descriptive of His Nature, and a third on His Power, which alone can give strength to mankind, this emphasis on God's absolute sovereignty continues. In chapters 43, 44, 45 and 46 it is perhaps especially abundant; yet there are few chapters without it.

Often it is emphasized by the repetition of practically identical statements:

I am God, and there is none else. I am God, and there is none like me. I am the Lord, your Holy One, the Creator of Israel, your King. I am the Lord; that is my name; and my glory will I not give to another. I am the Lord, and there is none else.

Imagery, in such abundance that it becomes at times almost naïve in its outbursts and in its variety, increases the emphasis of these many terse declarations; and figures of speech likewise abound. Birds, sheep, prisoners in darkness, cedars of Lebanon, the blind and the deaf, the hungry and the thirsty, smiths, carpenters, cities and islands, Babylon, "the lady of kingdoms," kings, queens, and princes, dragons and owls, deserts and forests, alien peoples of Egypt, of Ethiopia, of Chaldea, heathen gods, astrologers, star-gazers, women in travail, little children—all these animate and inanimate beings shall honour God as the one Lord of all. The similes and metaphors used by Isaiah of Babylon follow one another in the same swift succession. God shall feed his flock *like a shepherd;* He takes up the islands in His hand *as a very little thing;* He holds His people *like a polished arrow in His quiver;* He has written their names *as though on the palms of His hands;* He will make the wilderness of Zion *like the Garden of Eden;* His word is *like the rain and the snow from heaven;* He shall make the desert to blossom *as the rose;* the earth shall wax old *like a garment* and the heavens vanish *like smoke;* but His salvation shall be forever.

Such imagery and figures enhance these especial qualities of the poetry of this later Isaiah. They make the new *more* new; the old, forsaken knowledge *more* revered; the summons to awake, to hearken, and to sing *more* emphatic and exultant; and the Reality of God as the Lord of the whole earth *more* real.

As we read his beautiful words, his lines which rise with light and ring with ecstasy, we may well see in him more of a poet than a prophet. Yet we must never forget that he brought to Hebrew prophecy, at a time when the old empires were falling and the dawn of a new age in history seemed at hand, an imperishable hope, not only for the future of his own people, but of a world under the absolute domination of God. That Israel was not to see that new age for many more centuries and that her return home was darkened by disappointment and sorrow, do not dim the strength of his teaching or the ardour of his hope.

2

The last of our great prophets, Isaiah of Babylon, expressed by his genius the faith which, in spite of despair and of anguish, glowed in the minds of all his forerunners —a faith and a hope, dimmed sometimes by their barren deserts, their rough fields, their city streets, obscured by injustice and by moral wrong, yet never entirely darkened, since they, too, were the servants of God and knew His mercy and His righteousness as well as His just anger. Their words rang often with menace and reproof, with the necessity for punishment, destruction, and exile; yet could they have heard his own, they would have rejoiced with him in his larger, more confident hope. Not even Hosea and Jeremiah, or Isaiah of Jerusalem in his brighter hours, had seen that hope with his vision; yet they, too, had longed for it and dedicated all their powers to its realization. More gifted than all other prophets in his use of language, forever memorable for the astonishing wealth of his imagination and for his new understanding of God in His relation to the world of men, Isaiah of Babylon should be looked upon as the completion of prophetic desires, as the Old Testament fulfillment of all prophetic hope.

PART FOUR

Characteristic Selections
from the Prophets

READERS OF this book should understand that the *Selections* which follow are (1) merely illustrative of the work of each prophet and (2) at times necessarily repetitious since certain portions of several of them have already appeared in preceding chapters. I believe, however, that each selection is characteristic of its author; and I have given to each such notes and comments as may be helpful to its reading and study.

I hope that these excerpts and quotations may not only prove interesting and enlightening in themselves, but that they may lead to much further reading in the prophetic books from which they are chosen.

Except in cases where the language is unmistakably in prose (as in the vision of Isaiah of Jerusalem in the Temple) I have broken the lines into their poetic form, partly for easier reading, largely for uniformity.

1

From Amos

THIS FIRST selection from Amos is taken from the opening chapters of his book where he utters his oracles, first against neighbouring peoples and then against the kingdoms of Judah and Israel. The selection, slightly cut, begins with his prophecy against the chief Philistine cities, Gaza, Ashdod, Ashkelon, and Ekron, and continues with that against Ammon.

The prophet's use of repetition, refrain, irony, and climax should be especially noted as well as the strength and terseness of his style and his dominant atmosphere of anger and of doom.

Thus saith the Lord:
For three transgressions of Gaza, and for four,
I will not turn away the punishment thereof.
But I will send a fire on the wall of Gaza
Which shall devour the palaces thereof.
And I will cut off the inhabitant from Ashdod,
And him that holdeth the sceptre from Ashkelon,
And I will turn mine hand against Ekron;

And the remnant of the Philistines shall perish,
Saith the Lord God.

Thus saith the Lord:
For three transgressions of the children of Ammon, and for
*   four,*
I will not turn away the punishment thereof.
But, I will kindle a fire in the wall of Rabbah,
And it shall devour the palaces thereof,
With shouting in the day of battle,
With a tempest in the day of the whirlwind.
And their king shall go into captivity,
He and his princes together,
Saith the Lord.

Thus saith the Lord:
For three transgressions of Judah, and for four,
I will not turn away the punishment thereof;
Because they have despised the law of the Lord,
And have not kept his commandments.
But I will send a fire upon Judah,
And it shall devour the palaces of Jerusalem.

Thus saith the Lord:
For three transgressions of Israel, and for four,
I will not turn away the punishment thereof;
Because they sold the righteous for silver,
And the poor for a pair of shoes.
That pant after the dust of the earth on the head of the
*   poor*
And turn aside the way of the meek.
And a man and his father will go in unto the same maid
To profane my holy name.
Behold! I am pressed under you
As a cart is pressed that is full of sheaves.
Therefore the flight shall perish from the swift,

And the strong shall not strengthen his force,
Neither shall the mighty deliver himself.
And he that is courageous among the mighty
Shall flee away naked in that day,
Saith the Lord.

This second selection from Amos, taken from chapter 6 of his book, illustrates especially well his rage against the luxurious habits of both kingdoms of Israel. Perhaps more vividly than any of his addresses it echoes his relentless anger against the sinful practices of the rich.

Woe unto them that are at ease in Zion,
And trust in the mountain of Samaria,
Which are named chief of the nations
To whom the house of Israel came!
Ye that put far away the evil day
And cause the seat of violence to come near.
That lie upon beds of ivory,
And stretch themselves upon their couches,
And eat the lambs out of the flock
And the calves out of the midst of the stall;
That chant to the sound of the viol,
And invent to themselves instruments of music;
That drink wine in bowls
And anoint themselves with the chief ointments.

Therefore now shall they go captive,
And the banquet of them that stretched themselves shall be
     removed.
And it shall come to pass, if there remain ten men in one
     house,
That they shall die.
For, behold! the Lord commandeth,
And he will smite the great house with breaches,
And the little house with clefts.

This third selection from Amos is perhaps his most famous utterance, since it declares his understanding that God is not alone the God of Israel, but that His mercy has been shown in the past to people whom Israel has looked upon as her enemies. It may well be regarded as the conclusion of his prophetic messages.

Are ye not as children of the Ethiopians unto me,
O children of Israel?
Saith the Lord.
Have not I brought up Israel out of the land of Egypt?
And the Philistines from Caphtor?
And the Syrians from Kir?

2

From Hosea

IT IS DIFFICULT to select characteristic passages from Hosea, because, as we have already learned, his book is singularly lacking in unity. It is, instead, discursive, even disorderly, one verse following upon another with often little evidence of any close relationship. The selections chosen are, therefore, necessarily brief, and they have been made more upon the principle of style than of actual content. Each illustrates Hosea's manner of speaking, or of writing; each conveys his sense of sadness, and his assurance, in spite of Israel's idolatry, of God's ultimate mercy toward her; each contains the images and figures of speech characteristic of him.

The first selection, from chapter 13, expresses Hosea's sorrowful concern over Ephraim's idolatry and echoes as well the sorrow of God.

When Ephraim spake trembling,
He exalted himself in Israel;
But when he offended in Baal, he died.

And now they sin more and more,
And have made them molten images of their silver,
And idols according to their own understanding,
All of it the work of the craftsmen.

Therefore they shall be as the morning cloud,
And as the early dew that passeth away;
As the chaff that is driven with the whirlwind out of the floor,
And as the smoke out of the chimney.

Yet I am the Lord thy God from the land of Egypt,
And thou shall know no god but me;
For there is no saviour beside me.

The second selection reveals Hosea as capable of anger as well as of mercy. It is taken from chapter 7, and in its description of the wrath of God is perhaps the most threatening and ruthless of all Hosea's prophecies.

When I would have healed Israel,
Then the iniquity of Ephraim was discovered,
And the wickedness of Samaria.
For they commit falsehood, and the thief cometh in,
And the troop of robbers spoileth without.
Their own doings have beset them about;
They are before my face.
They make the king glad with their wickedness,
And the princes with their lies.
They are all hot as an oven, and have devoured their judges.
All their kings are fallen,
There is none among them that calleth unto me.

Ephraim is like a silly dove without heart.
They call to Egypt; they go to Assyria.
When they shall go, I will spread my net upon them,
I will bring them down as the fowls of heaven.

Woe unto them! For they have fled from me.
Destruction unto them! because they have transgressed
against me.
Though I have redeemed them, yet they have spoken lies
against me.

The final selection from Hosea is the one most truly characteristic of him, both in manner and in material. Its verses open chapter 6 and are seemingly spoken by a repentant people, whose only hope is in God.

Come, and let us return unto the Lord;
For he hath torn, and he will heal us,
He hath smitten, and he will bind us up.
After two days will he revive us,
In the third day he will raise us up,
And we shall live in his sight.
Then shall we know, if we follow on to know the Lord;
His going forth is prepared as the morning;
And he shall come unto us as the rain,
As the latter and former rain unto the earth.

3

From Isaiah of Jerusalem

IN THESE THREE selections from Isaiah of Jerusalem
I have tried to show still further the unique variety of
his writings, his unsurpassed power in the use of language.
The first passage, in prose, describes his vision in the Temple at Jerusalem; the second from chapter 5 is his beautiful
and moving song of God's vineyard, in its complete form;
the third, which comes from the first chapter of his book,
though it is without doubt later in composition than the
other two selections, expresses in most vivid words, phrases,
and figures the miserable state of sinfulness into which
Judah and Jerusalem have fallen and the desolation which
must be their punishment.

(I)

*In the year that King Uzziah died I saw also the Lord
sitting upon a throne, high and lifted up, and his train
filled the temple.*

*Above it stood the seraphim. Each one had six wings.
With twain he covered his face, and with twain he covered*

*his feet, and with twain he did fly. And one cried unto
another and said: Holy, holy, holy is the Lord of hosts!
The whole earth is full of his glory.*

*And the posts of the door moved at the voice of him
that cried, and the house was filled with smoke.*

*Then said I: Woe is me! For I am undone; because I
am a man of unclean lips, and I dwell in the midst of a
people of unclean lips. For mine eyes have seen the King,
the Lord of hosts.*

*Then flew one of the seraphim unto me, having a live
coal in his hand which he had taken with the tongs from
off the altar. And he laid it upon my mouth and said: Lo,
this hath touched thy lips; and thine iniquity is taken away,
and thy sin purged.*

*Also I heard the voice of the Lord saying: Whom shall
I send, and who will go for us?*

Then said I: Here am I. Send me.

(2)

*Now will I sing to my well-beloved
A song of my beloved touching his vineyard:*

*My well-beloved hath a vineyard in a very fruitful hill.
And he fenced it,
And gathered out the stones thereof,
And planted it with the choicest vine,
And built a tower in the midst of it,
And also made a wine-press therein.
And he looked that it should bring forth grapes,
And it brought forth wild grapes.*

And now, O inhabitants of Jerusalem and men of Judah,
Judge, I pray you, betwixt me and my vineyard.
What could have been done more to my vineyard
That I have not done in it?
Wherefore, when I looked that it should bring forth grapes,
Brought it forth wild grapes?

And now, go to! I will tell you what I will do to my vine-
*   yard.*
I will take away the hedge thereof,
And it shall be eaten up.
And break down the wall thereof,
And it shall be trodden down.
And I will lay it waste;
It shall not be pruned, nor digged;
But there shall come up briers and thorns.
I will also command the clouds
That they rain no rain upon it.

For the vineyard of the Lord of hosts is the house of Israel,
And the men of Judah his pleasant plant.
And he looked for judgment, but behold! oppression;
For righteousness, but behold! a cry.

(3)

Hear, O heavens, and give ear, O earth,
For the Lord hath spoken:

I have nourished and brought up children,
And they have rebelled against me.
The ox knoweth his owner
And the ass his master's crib;
But Israel doth not know,
My people doth not consider.

Ah, sinful nation, a people laden with iniquity,
A seed of evildoers, children that are corrupters,

They have provoked the Holy One of Israel unto anger,
They are gone away backward.

Your country is desolate, your cities are burned with fire,
Your land, strangers devour it in your presence,
And it is desolate, as overthrown by strangers.
And the daughter of Zion is left as a cottage in a vine-
    yard,
As a lodge in a garden of cucumbers,
As a besieged city.

4

From Micah

THE ONE SELECTION given here from Micah is composed of verses from the first three chapters of his book, chapters that, according to many scholars, are all which we can be sure *actually* belong to him. In his portrait as given in Part II of this book we have already become familiar with his definition of true religion, whether or not it was truly spoken or written by him. In the verses which follow readers can discern those social sins which he most deplored and hated, those unjust acts of the rich against the poor, always his friends. They can discern also his righteous rage against these acts of oppression and violence.

Hear, all ye people!
Hearken, O earth, and all that therein is!
And let the Lord God be witness against you,
The Lord from his holy temple!

Woe to them that devise iniquity
And work evil upon their beds!
When the morning is light, they practise it
Because it is in the power of their hand.

They covet fields, and take them by violence;
And houses and take them away.
So they oppress a man and his house,
Even a man and his heritage.

And I said, Hear, I pray you, O heads of Jacob,
And ye princes of the house of Israel!
Is it not for you to know judgment?
Who hate the good and love the evil,
Who pluck off their skin from off them,
And their flesh from off their bones.
Who also eat the flesh of my people
And flay their skin from them;
And they break their bones and chop them in pieces
As for the pot, and as flesh within the cauldron.

They shall cry unto the Lord, but he will not hear them:
He will hide his face from them at that time
Because they have behaved themselves ill in their doings.

5

From Jeremiah

IN THE CHOICE of these four selections from Jeremiah, who really demands an extra number in order that his contrasting, even conflicting moods be made clear, I have tried to show his own many-sided nature as well as that of his utterances.

The first selection is taken from chapter 20 and echoes Jeremiah's despair, his faithlessness and yet his faith.

> *O Lord, thou hast deceived me, and I was deceived.*
> *Thou art stronger than I, and hast prevailed.*
> *I am in derision daily; every one mocketh me.*
> *Then I said: I will not make mention of him*
> *Nor speak any more in his name.*
> *But his word was in mine heart*
> *As a burning fire shut up in my bones,*
> *And I was weary with forbearing,*
> *And I could not stay.*
>
> *But the Lord is with me as a mighty, terrible one;*
> *Therefore my persecutors shall stumble,*
> *And they shall not prevail.*

They shall be greatly ashamed,
For they shall not prosper,
Their everlasting confusion shall never be forgotten.

Sing unto the Lord, praise ye the Lord:
For he hath delivered the soul of the poor
From the hand of evildoers.

The second selection, from chapters 7 and 8, is from the many oracles of Jeremiah against the idolatrous people of Judah. In it his forceful, scornful words illustrate well his use of imagery to convey his awful message.

Cut off thine hair, O Jerusalem, and cast it away,
And take up a lamentation on high places.
For the Lord hath rejected and forsaken the generation of
*   his wrath.*
For the children of Judah have done evil in my sight,
Saith the Lord.
They have set their abominations in the house that is called
*   by my name.*
And the carcasses of this people shall be meat for the fowls
*   of the air*
And for the beasts of the earth.

Then I will cause to cease from the cities of Judah
And from the streets of Jerusalem
The voice of the bridegroom, and the voice of the bride,
For the land shall be desolate.

The third selection is taken from the unique letter, in chapter 29, which Jeremiah wrote to the captives taken by Nebuchadnezzar to Babylon. In this letter he gives not only advice for their life in Babylon, but also the promises of God for their return home, once they have repented of their sins and turned again to Him.

Build ye houses and dwell in them;
And plant gardens, and eat the fruit of them.
Take ye wives, and beget sons and daughters;
And take wives for your sons,
And give your daughters to husbands
That ye may be increased there and not diminished.
And seek the peace of the city
Whither I have caused you to be carried away captives;
And pray unto the Lord for it,
For in the peace thereof shall ye have peace.

For thus saith the Lord:
After seventy years be accomplished at Babylon
I will visit you,
And perform my good word toward you.
And ye shall seek me and find me
When ye shall search for me with all your heart.
And I will turn away your captivity,
And I will bring you again to the place
Whence I caused you to be carried away captive.

The fourth selection, perhaps the most beautiful of all Jeremiah's writings, describes the New Covenant which God will make with all His people of a united Israel. It is taken from chapters 31 and 33 of his book and expresses his imperishable hope in the repentance of his people and in their ultimate future.

Behold! the days come, saith the Lord
That I will make a New Covenant with the house of Israel
And with the house of Judah:
Not according to the covenant that I made with their
    fathers
In the day that I took them by the hand
To bring them out of the land of Egypt,
Which covenant they broke

Although I was an husband unto them,
Saith the Lord.
But this shall be the Covenant I will make with the house of
Israel:
After those days, I will put my law in their inward parts,
And write it in their hearts:
And I will be their God,
And they shall be my people;
And they shall all know me
From the least of them unto the greatest of them,
Saith the Lord.
For I will forgive their iniquity,
And I will remember their sin no more.

Thus saith the Lord of hosts:
Again in this place, which is desolate
Without man and without beast,
And in all the cities thereof;
In the cities of the mountains,
In the cities of the vale,
And in the cities of the south,
And in the land of Benjamin,
And in the places about Jerusalem,
And in the cities of Judah,
Shall be a habitation of shepherds,
Causing their flocks to lie down.
Again there shall be heard in this place
The voice of joy, and the voice of gladness,
The voice of the bridegroom, and the voice of the bride;
The voice of them that shall say,
Praise the Lord of hosts!
For the Lord is good,
For his mercy endureth for ever.

6

From Isaiah of Babylon

O F ALL OUR six prophets, Isaiah of Babylon is most
baffling and difficult when one attempts to select
characteristic passages from his work. The chapter about
him as a poet gives the outstanding themes and subjects
which claimed his incomparable imagination and suggests
at its beginning an uninterrupted reading of his chapters.
The passages which follow have been chosen largely because they possess that unity which makes it possible to see
them easily as single poems. Each illustrates this Isaiah's
power over language; his sense of climax; his wealth of
imagery; and the musical, exultant quality always evident
in his verse.

The first selection, to which we might give the title *The
Power of God*, forms the conclusion to chapter 40.

To whom then will ye liken me,
Or shall I be equal?
Saith the Holy One.
Lift up your eyes on high
And behold! who hath created these things,

That bringeth out their host by number.
He calleth them all by names by the greatness of his might,
For that he is strong in power, not one faileth.
Why sayest thou, O Jacob, and speakest, O Israel,
My way is hid from the Lord,
And my judgment is passed over from my God?
Hast thou not known? hast thou not heard
That the everlasting God, the Lord,
The Creator of the ends of the earth,
Fainteth not, neither is weary?
There is no searching of his understanding.
He giveth power to the faint,
And to them that have no might he increaseth strength.
Even the youths shall faint and be weary,
And the young men shall utterly fall.
But they that wait upon the Lord shall renew their strength;
They shall mount up with wings as eagles.
They shall run and not be weary.
They shall walk, and not faint.

The second poem comes from chapter 41. In its ecstatic, concrete symbolism it might well be called *God's Care for the Helpless.*

When the poor and the needy seek water,
And there is none,
And their tongue faileth for thirst,
I, the Lord, will hear them,
I, the God of Israel, will not forsake them.
I will open rivers in high places,
And fountains in the midst of the valleys.
I will make the wilderness a pool of water,
And the dry land springs of water.
I will plant in the wilderness the cedar,
The shittah tree, and the myrtle, and the oil tree.
I will set in the desert the fir tree,
And the pine, and the box tree together.

That they may see, and know,
And consider, and understand together
That the hand of the Lord hath done this
And the Holy One of Israel hath created it.

The third poem by Isaiah of Babylon is chosen from chapter 43 and is perhaps the most beautifully expressed of all his many poems about God as the Redeemer of His people.

But now, saith the Lord that created thee, O Jacob,
And he that formed thee, O Israel:
Fear not, for I have redeemed thee.
I have called thee by thy name; thou art mine.
When thou passest through the waters, I will be with thee;
And through the rivers, they shall not overflow thee.
When thou walkest through the fire, thou shalt not be
*   burned,*
Neither shall the flame kindle upon thee.
For I am the Lord, thy God,
The Holy One of Israel, thy Saviour.
I gave Egypt for thy ransom,
Ethiopia and Seba for thee.
Since thou wast precious in my sight,
Thou hast been honourable, and I have loved thee.
Therefore will I give men for thee
And people for thy life.
Fear not, for I am with thee.
I will bring thy seed from the east,
And gather thee from the west;
I will say to the north, Give up,
And to the south, Keep not back.
Bring my sons from far,
And my daughters from the ends of the earth;
Even every one that is called by my name.
For I created him for my glory.

Ye are my witnesses, saith the Lord,
And my servant whom I have chosen,
That ye may know, and believe me,
And understand that I am he.
Before me there was no God formed
Neither shall there be after me.
I, even I, am the Lord,
And beside me there is no Saviour.

Selected Books on Prophecy
and the Prophets

These books about prophecy and the prophets are purposely few in number and most carefully selected. I have named only those which I know will prove both valuable and interesting.

1

The four books which I am recommending above all others are as lively and engaging as they are basic and revealing. Every one of them will prove of immense value to all readers who want to know more about the prophets of ancient Israel. They are:

The Old Testament Prophets, by E. W. Heaton, 1958. This book can be obtained, bound in paper, in Pelican or in Penguin Books. In Pelican form it has to be ordered from England; in Penguin form it can be bought in this country. It is not only extremely valuable, but every page of it is clear and fascinating. Small wonder that in its first edition, 1949, the two leading English newspapers, *The London Times* and *The Manchester Guardian,* praised it to the skies.

Everyday Life in Old Testament Times, also by E. W. Heaton, Scribner's, 1956. This book, which should be read by every person interested in the Old Testament, does not deal primarily with the prophets. It is, instead, a fascinating and illustrated portrayal of life as it was lived in Old Testament times. In its final chapter, however, it describes religious life; and the concluding pages of that chapter define briefly, yet most admirably, the faith of the prophets. I recommend this book most enthusiastically.

The Relevance of the Prophets, by R. B. Y. Scott, Macmillan, 1944. From beginning to end this is a wonderful book, as readable as it is revealing. No one who is interested in the prophets should miss it.

Personalities of the Old Testament, by Fleming James, Scribner's, 1939. Although this is not a new book, its value and appeal are perennial. Readers who want to know more about the prophets as individuals will find that knowledge here. It affords unqualified enjoyment in every chapter.

I cannot too strongly urge the reading, and the *ownership,* of these four books.

2

Next to these four indispensables, I would recommend portions of other books:

In *The Old Testament and Modern Study,* edited by H. H. Rowley, 1951, and now to be obtained in an Oxford University Press paperback, 1961, there is a fine chapter entitled "Prophetic Literature," Chapter V.

In *Theology of the Old Testament,* Vol. I, by Walther Eichrodt, Westminster Press, Philadelphia, 1961, there is in Chapter VIII an excellent treatment of Classical Prophecy, together with material on its backgrounds.

In *The Prophets and the Rise of Judaism,* by Adolph Lods, London, 1947, there is, especially in Book II of Part I, a first-class presentation of the great prophets.

In *Great Ages and Ideas of the Jewish People,* edited by Leo W. Schwarz, Random House, 1956, the third chapter gives a fine study of Classical Prophecy.

In two remarkable books on the Old Testament there are most valuable pages on the prophets, together with their historical backgrounds. These books are: *Introduction to the Old Testament,* by Robert H. Pfeiffer, first issued by Harper in 1941 and often re-issued, and *A Light to the Nations,* by Norman Gottwald, Harper, 1959. These are the best books I know on the Old Testament as a whole.

3

There are two very recent books which will possess great value for those readers eager to know the *latest* words and ideas on any really important subject. One of these is given to a thorough and fascinating study of the institutions of ancient Israel; the other is devoted entirely to the prophets.

The first of these books, one which for me has provided hours, even days of complete absorption and pleasure, is *Ancient Israel,* by Roland de Vaux, O.P., McGraw-Hill, 1961. The second, which gives perhaps the most thorough, even exhaustive presentation of the Hebrew prophets from every conceivable angle, is *The Prophets,* by Abraham Heschel, Jewish Publication Society of America, 1962.

4

Nor in any list of suggested books should one omit the admirable twelve volumes of *The Interpreter's Bible,* which may, of course, be found in any good library and which will hold the full attention of the intelligent reader for hours on end. The only problem will be to leave them!

In the volumes of this wonderful commentary, which gives the Biblical text of both the Authorized and the Revised Standard Versions, there are excellent articles by the best authorities on the individual prophets. Volume V treats the Isaiahs and Jeremiah; Volume VI presents Amos, Hosea, and Micah. These accounts are detailed and most valuable; and each is accompanied by a bibliography.